MICHEL GUÉRARD'S CUISINE FOR HOME COOKS

by Michel Guérard

Translated and Annotated by
Judith Hill and Tina Ujlaki

WILLIAM MORROW AND COMPANY, INC., NEW YORK

Portions of this book were originally published
in French under the titles
La Grande Cuisine Minceur, copyright © 1976,
La Cuisine Gourmande, copyright © 1978,
and *Mes Recettes de la Télévision: La Cuisine Légère*,
copyright © 1982 by Editions Robert Laffont, S.A.

Library of Congress Cataloging in Publication Data

Guérard, Michel, 1933-
Michel Guérard's Cuisine for home cooks.

Includes index.
1. Cookery, French.   I. Hill, Judith.   II. Ujlaki,
Tina.   III. Title.   IV. Title: Cuisine for home cooks.
TX719.G8165   1984   641.5   83-17247
ISBN 0-688-02658-3

Printed in the United States of America

First U.S. Edition

1 2 3 4 5 6 7 8 9 10

BOOK DESIGN BY JAMES UDELL

PREFACE

Chefs have a way of preferring the role of host, rather than being the guests of others. And they are often unwilling to disclose the secrets of their culinary inventions. Michel Guérard is a man of quite opposite temperament. For four years, with faithful regularity, he appeared in the homes of the French public bearing bouquets of his personal recipes. It was, of course, *la télévision* that allowed this gregarious three-star celebrity to make his entrance into the living rooms of France.

The mail that poured in after each broadcast continued in a rising flood as the months went by. The program provoked rapt attention from novice cooks and skilled ones and from fellow professionals. Chef Guérard clearly was providing a welcome service and making a rousing good show of it.

The task of satisfying the most knowledgeable gastronomic audience in the world could have been difficult; everyone from housewives with neither the skills nor the time for complicated recipes to the sophisticated elite of the three-star circuit was watching him. But as it turned out, the challenge suited Michel Guérard perfectly. The recipes he developed for the TV program were simple, often of an informal genre, and relied on methods familiar to any cook. With his extraordinary sense of taste and gift for combining flavors and ingredients, he easily made many new, approachable dishes with all of his accustomed three-star quality.

Requests came, too, for some of the famous recipes from his books *La grande cuisine minceur* and his masterwork *La cuisine gourmande* to be demonstrated on the show. From these sources came more recipes that fit the program's formula for simplicity. Though the *minceur* repertory is often notably tricky to execute and many *gourmande* recipes climb to Olympian heights, in parts of both those collections Guérard had already proven something: That it also takes a great chef to devise recipes that are *both* simple and perfect.

The television collection was eventually expanded into this carefully selected book for home cooks. It is only partly a book for daily fare. Michel Guérard rightly assumes that cooking is something one does for friends, to be festive, for the love of it. Here and there he presents culinary challenges—but he keeps well away from the demands of a restaurant kitchen. His selections are an ideal introduction to the imagination of this world-famous chef.

EDITORS' NOTES

In the course of translating and testing the recipes in this country, we came up with bits of advice for American readers which are printed as **NOTES** *followed by information printed in italics.* Other **NOTES** printed in regular type are Michel Guérard's own remarks.

⁋ NOTE: Look for this symbol preceding some **NOTES** indicating that a recipe may be prepared ahead up to that point.

J.H. & T.U.

CONTENTS

Les soupes

SOUPS

Crème de pois frais

Cream of Pea Soup

To serve 4:

2	tablespoons butter
1	onion, chopped
1	head tender lettuce, such as Bibb, torn into pieces
1½	quarts chicken stock *(pages 194–195)*
2	cups fresh or frozen tiny green peas
⅔	cup *crème fraîche (page 206)*
	Salt and pepper

Melt the butter in a saucepan, add the onion, and sauté it until lightly browned. Add the lettuce and cook it until wilted, about 4 minutes. Add the chicken stock and bring to a boil. Then add the peas and simmer for 6 minutes if frozen, 15 minutes if fresh.

Purée the soup in a food processor or an electric blender and strain back into the saucepan.

❡ **NOTE:** *The recipe can be prepared ahead to this point. Ed.*

Reheat the soup and bring it to a boil. Whisk in the *crème fraîche* and bring the soup to a boil again. Season to taste with salt and pepper and serve in heated soup bowls or individual tureens.

Crème d'oseille mousseuse minceur

Minceur Cream of Sorrel Soup

To serve 4:

2   teaspoons olive oil

2   garlic cloves, crushed

¼   pound fresh sorrel, chopped

Salt and pepper

1   quart chicken stock *(pages 194–195)*

2   eggs

Heat the olive oil in a medium-size saucepan over moderate heat, add the garlic, and cook until it begins to brown. Add the chopped sorrel and salt and pepper and stir until the sorrel is wilted. Then add the stock and simmer for 15 minutes. Purée the soup in a food processor or an electric blender. Return it to the saucepan and keep warm.

In a medium-size bowl, whisk the eggs until they double in volume. Gradually pour them into the hot—but not close to boiling—soup, whisking rapidly. Continue whisking until the egg has lightly thickened the soup. Taste and add salt or pepper if needed, pour the soup into heated soup bowls or individual tureens, and serve immediately.

Soupe de tomates fraîches au pistou minceur

Minceur Fresh Tomato Soup with Basil

To serve 4:

1   teaspoon olive oil

1   medium carrot, sliced

½   leek, white part only, well washed and sliced

1   shallot, sliced

1   garlic clove, chopped

    Sprig thyme

½   bay leaf

1   cup chopped fresh tomatoes *(page 204)*

1   tablespoon tomato paste

5   cups chicken stock *(pages 194–195)* or water

    Salt and pepper

    Pistou: About 2 tablespoons fresh basil leaves ground to a paste in a small mortar with 1 teaspoon olive oil

In a saucepan, heat the olive oil, add the carrot, leek, shallot, and garlic, and cook gently until they give off some of their liquid. Then add the thyme and bay leaf, tomatoes, tomato paste, chicken stock or water, and salt and pepper. Simmer, partially covered, over moderate heat for 20 minutes.

Remove the thyme and bay leaf. Purée the soup in a food processor or an electric blender and then strain it back into the saucepan. Make the *pistou.* Reheat the soup and check the seasoning. Pour it into soup bowls or individual tureens and at the last moment add a quarter of the *pistou* to each serving.

NOTE: This is a delicious hot soup, but it is also particularly good served chilled in the summertime. Store in the refrigerator after straining and taste for seasoning before serving. After adding the *pistou,* float a small leaf of fresh basil on the top of each serving.

Potage froid de poireaux et pommes de terre à la crème

Cold Potato and Leek Soup with Cream

To serve 4 as a first course or 2 as a summer supper:

1½	tablespoons butter
1	small onion, finely chopped
2	leeks, white part only, well washed and finely chopped
3	cups chicken stock *(pages 194–195)*
¾	pound waxy potatoes
	Salt
1	cup heavy cream
	Cayenne pepper
1	tablespoon chopped chives or fresh chervil leaves

In a large saucepan, melt the butter and add the chopped onion and leeks. Cook them gently until softened but not browned. Add the chicken stock and bring to a boil. Peel and dice the potatoes and add them to the saucepan. Add a little salt and cook the soup until the potatoes are tender, about 25 minutes. Cool the soup and then refrigerate it until well chilled.

❡ NOTE: *The recipe can be prepared ahead to this point. Ed.*

Just before serving, add the cream to the soup and stir well. For a frothier soup, whip the cream lightly before adding it to the soup. Add a little cayenne pepper and salt to taste. Ladle the soup into cups or bowls and garnish with the chopped chives or chervil leaves.

NOTE: For a summer supper, this soup becomes a meal in itself. Serve it with the following accompaniment: Brush slices of crusty whole-grain bread with olive oil, toast them under the broiler, and then rub with a garlic clove. Cover the toasted bread with chopped fresh tomatoes (*page 204*), season with salt, sprinkle with chopped fresh herbs, and top each with a couple of cooked asparagus spears.

Soupe de moules

Mussel Soup

To serve 4 as a first course or 2 as a light supper:

½	cup white wine
2	pounds mussels, bearded and scrubbed
¼	cup olive oil
1	onion, chopped
1	leek, white part only, well washed and chopped
1	medium carrot, finely diced
1	garlic clove, chopped
⅔	cup chopped fresh tomatoes (*page 204*)
	Bouquet garni
2	cups chicken stock (*pages 194–195*)
	Salt and pepper
⅔	cup heavy cream

In a large saucepan, bring the white wine and the mussels to a boil. Cover tightly, reduce the heat to moderate, and cook until the shells have opened, about 5 minutes. When the mussels are cool enough to handle, shell them into a soup tureen. Cover them with parchment paper to keep them warm. Strain the mussel broth through a strainer lined with a double thickness of cheesecloth into a bowl.

In another saucepan, heat the olive oil and add the onion, leek, and carrot. Cook gently, uncovered, until the vegetables are soft, 10 to 15 minutes. Then add the garlic, tomatoes, bouquet garni, chicken stock, reserved mussel broth, and salt. Bring to a boil, skim the surface to remove any scum, and cover the saucepan. Simmer the soup for 30 minutes.

After 30 minutes, uncover the soup, remove the bouquet garni, and whisk in the cream. Add salt (sparingly) and pepper to taste and return the soup to a boil. Remove the parchment paper covering the mussels in the tureen and pour in the hot soup.

NOTE: In the summertime, this soup can be served chilled. If so, a few drops of vinegar might be added.

Les entrées froides

COLD APPETIZERS

Oeuf glacé à la ratatouille minceur

Minceur Ratatouille and Eggs Glazed with Aspic

To serve 4:

Ratatouille niçoise *(page 147)*

Vinegar (for acidulating the poaching water)

4   eggs

1½   teaspoons (½ package) gelatine

1   cup cold chicken stock *(pages 194–195)*

1   tablespoon fresh chervil leaves *(see page 212 for substitution)*

Make the ratatouille and refrigerate it.

Fill a shallow saucepan ¾ full of water and add about 3 tablespoons vinegar per quart of water. Bring the acidulated water to a bare simmer. Break the eggs into the simmering water and poach them until the whites are just set, about 4 minutes. With a slotted spoon, lift out the eggs and transfer them to paper towels. Trim away any ragged edges and leave to cool.

Soften the gelatine in the cold chicken stock until spongy, about 5 minutes. Pour this mixture into a small saucepan set over extremely low heat and stir until the gelatine dissolves completely. Chill this aspic until it is syrupy, about 15 minutes. *(**NOTE:** If the gelatine sets too much, simply melt it over extremely low heat and chill again until set to the proper consistency. Ed.)*

Place the eggs on a wire rack set over a pan to catch the drips. Then, with a spoon, mask each egg with a little of the aspic, refrigerate the eggs until the layer of aspic sets, and repeat this procedure 2 or 3 times until the eggs are nicely glazed.

Spoon a bed of ratatouille onto each of 4 chilled plates, put an egg in the middle, and decorate with the chervil leaves.

Le mille-feuille au roquefort

Roquefort Napoleons

To serve 4 to 6:

¾ pound puff pastry *(page 207)* or buy the
    pastry *(page 212)*

2   ounces roquefort cheese, crumbled (about ⅓
    cup)

6   tablespoons *fromage blanc (page 206)*

¾ cup heavy cream

2   tablespoons armagnac or brandy

    Salt and pepper

1   tablespoon chopped chives

Preheat the oven to 425° F.

Lightly flour a work surface and roll out the puff pastry to measure 19 inches long, 9 inches wide, and ⅛ inch thick. Cut the edges to even them and then cut this rectangle into thirds to form smaller rectangles, each measuring about 6 by 8 inches.

Sprinkle a baking sheet lightly with water and put the 3 pastry rectangles on it. Prick the pastry thoroughly, every half inch or so, with the tines of a fork to prevent it from rising too much. Bake the pastry in the preheated oven until nicely browned, about 15 minutes. (**NOTE:** *The pastry must be completely cooked, but if it threatens to burn, reduce the oven heat, and continue to bake until crisp throughout. Ed.)* Transfer the pastry to a rack.

While the pastry cools, prepare the filling. Combine the roquefort and the *fromage blanc* in a bowl. In another bowl, combine the heavy cream with the armagnac or brandy and beat together until the cream is lightly whipped. Then fold ¾ of the whipped cream into the cheese mixture and season with salt and pepper.

❨ **NOTE:** *The recipe can be prepared ahead to this point. Ed.*

ASSEMBLY:

With a spatula, spread one half of the cheese mixture over the first pastry rectangle. Cover with a second rectangle and spread the remaining cheese mixture over it. Top with the final pastry rectangle. Spread the reserved whipped cream over this top layer and sprinkle with the chopped chives. With a serrated knife, carefully cut the assembled napoleon into 4 to 6 slices.

Saumon à l'oeuf en gelée

Salmon-Rolled Poached Eggs in Aspic

To serve 4:

	Vinegar (for acidulating the poaching water)
4	eggs
	Zest of ½ lemon, cut in fine julienne strips
1½	teaspoons (½ package) gelatine
1	cup cold fish stock *(pages 196–197)*
4	thin slices smoked salmon
4	sprigs fresh dill or chervil
4	teaspoons chopped fresh tomatoes *(page 204)*
	Watercress sprigs (optional)

Fill a shallow saucepan ¾ full of water and add about 3 tablespoons vinegar per quart of water. Bring the acidulated water to a bare simmer. Break the eggs into the simmering water and poach them until the whites are just set, about 4 minutes. With a slotted spoon, lift out the eggs and transfer them to paper towels. Trim away any ragged edges and leave to cool.

In a small saucepan of boiling water, blanch the julienned lemon zest for 5 minutes, drain, rinse under cold water, and set aside.

Soften the gelatine in the cold fish stock until spongy, about 5 minutes. Pour this mixture into a small saucepan set over extremely low heat and stir until the gelatine dissolves completely. Chill this aspic until it is syrupy, about 15 minutes. (NOTE: *If the gelatine sets too much, simply melt it over extremely low heat and chill again until set to the proper consistency. Ed.)*

Wrap each of the poached eggs in a slice of smoked salmon. Place the wrapped eggs, seam side down, on a wire rack set over a pan to catch the drips. Decorate the wrapped eggs with the lemon zest, the sprigs of fresh dill or chervil, and the chopped tomatoes. Lightly coat the decorated eggs with the thickened aspic and refrigerate them until the aspic has set completely.

To serve, place an egg on each plate and garnish, if you like, with fresh watercress sprigs.

Rillettes aux deux saumons

Fresh and Smoked Salmon Rillettes

To serve 4 to 6:

⅔   pound salmon fillet

2   cups simple court-bouillon *(page 199)*

1   teaspoon finely chopped lemon zest

5   ounces butter, softened

2   egg yolks

4   teaspoons olive oil

1   tablespoon lemon juice

¼   cup heavy cream

¼   pound smoked salmon, thinly sliced

1   tablespoon chopped fresh chervil *(see page 212 for substitution)*

1   tablespoon chopped fresh tarragon *(see page 212 for substitution)*

Salt and pepper

2½- to 3-cup crock or terrine

Poach the fresh salmon fillet in the court-bouillon for 5 minutes. Remove it with a slotted spoon and let it cool.

In a small saucepan of boiling water, blanch the chopped lemon zest for 5 minutes, drain, and rinse under cold water.

In a large bowl, beat into the softened butter, first the egg yolks, one at a time, then the olive oil, followed by the lemon juice, and finally the cream. (**NOTE:** *These ingredients are most easily incorporated into the butter with an electric beater. Ed.)* Flake the poached salmon and stir it into the butter mixture. Cut the smoked salmon slices into ¼-inch dice and add them to the bowl with the herbs and lemon zest. Fold together until thoroughly mixed. Season well with salt and pepper. Pack the rillettes into the crock or terrine, smooth the surface, and refrigerate until firm.

Serve the chilled rillettes with toast. The rillettes could also be accompanied by a garnish of diced lemon: Cut the entire peel including the pith from a lemon, cut the pulp away from the membrane in sections, and then dice the pulp.

"Hure" de saumon au citron et au poivre vert minceur

Minceur Salmon Aspic with Lemon and Green Peppercorns

To serve 10:

1   pound salmon fillet

1   cup white wine

1   cup fish stock *(pages 196–197)*

2 tablespoons chopped parsley

Salt and pepper

3 eggs

5 lemons

4-ounce jar pimientos, drained and cut into small dice

4 tablespoons drained green peppercorns

2 shallots, finely chopped

2 teaspoons each chopped fresh tarragon and chervil *(see page 212 for substitutions)*

CLARIFIED FISH ASPIC:

1 onion

1 leek, white part only, well washed

3-inch piece of celery

2 mushrooms

1 tomato

¼ pound ground beef with no fat

4 teaspoons lemon juice

2 teaspoons dried tarragon

1 tablespoon chopped fresh chervil *(see page 212 for substitution)*

Salt and pepper

2 egg whites, lightly beaten

1 quart fish stock *(pages 196–197)*

2½ tablespoons (2½ envelopes) gelatine

A 1½-quart oblong ceramic or porcelain mold, 6 inches long, 3½ inches wide, and 4 inches deep

NOTE: Hure *is the word used for the pig's head from which a* charcutier *(pork butcher) makes jellied headcheese, hence by extension is used here to describe the salmon aspic made in a* charcutier's *oblong mold. Ed.*

Put the mold in the refrigerator.

Cut the salmon into strips about ¾ inch thick and ¾ inch wide. Marinate them in a flameproof baking dish with the white wine, 1 cup fish stock, parsley, and salt and pepper for 1 hour.

Boil the eggs for 8 minutes, cool them under cold running water, and shell. Separate the yolks and whites and chop them separately.

Poach the salmon for 2 or 3 minutes, no more; simply put the baking dish over direct heat, and bring the marinade to a simmer. Drain the fish on a dry cloth. Remove any fat and remaining bits of skin.

Peel the lemons, removing all the white pith. Cut the lemons into small dice, discarding as many of the membranes as possible and drain.

CLARIFIED FISH ASPIC:

Cut the onion, leek, celery, mushrooms, and tomato into pieces. Put the vegetables in the saucepan and add the ground beef, lemon juice, tarragon, chervil, salt and pepper, and the egg whites. Stir in the fish stock, bring the mixture to a simmer, and cook for 20 minutes.

NOTE: Added to the fish stock and vegetables, the whites of egg coagulate when the mixture is heated and rise to the surface in a thick layer to which small floating particles will cling, thus clarifying the stock. This process, however, depletes the flavor and aroma of the stock; the ground beef is added during the clarifying to compensate for the loss.

Soak the gelatine in a little water until it is soft. Add it to the simmering stock and stir until it is completely dissolved. Taste for seasoning.

Line a strainer with a damp cloth, set over a bowl, and slowly pour in the hot aspic. Chill the aspic until it is syrupy, about 15 minutes.

While filling the mold, the aspic in the bowl must be kept cool and at the consistency of oil or syrup—just at the point of setting. Have ready the strips of salmon and the rest of the ingredients.

Pour a small ladleful of aspic into the chilled mold and sprinkle with a little of the chopped whites and yolks, diced lemon and pimientos, green peppercorns, shallots, tarragon, and chervil. Arrange a few strips of salmon, lengthwise, over them. Return the mold to the refrigerator until this layer of aspic has just set. Repeat the procedure, one layer at a time, until all the ingredients have been used, ending with a layer of aspic. Cover the mold and chill in the refrigerator overnight.

To serve, dip the bottom of the mold briefly in hot water and unmold onto a chilled platter; or serve the *"hure" de saumon* directly from the mold. Cut it into slices ½ inch thick.

Sardines glacées au vin rouge

Marinated Sardines

To serve 4:

MARINADE:

2	cups red wine
⅔	cup red-wine vinegar
2	medium carrots, thinly sliced
1	medium onion, thinly sliced
	Bouquet garni
3	whole cloves
16	medium-size (about 1 pound in all) fresh sardines, dressed *(see **NOTE** for substitutions)*
	Salt and pepper
2	lemons
1	tablespoon fresh chervil leaves *(see page 212 for substitutions)*
1½	cups fresh tomato sauce *(page 201)*

NOTE: *Small Atlantic or blueback herring, pilchards, sprats, chubs, smelts, and fresh anchovies all work well for this recipe. Just be sure they weigh about 1 ounce each. Ed.*

MARINADE:

Put all of the marinade ingredients into a heavy saucepan and bring to a boil. Turn down the heat and simmer until reduced by one fourth. Transfer the marinade to a shallow, attractive, heatproof serving dish and let the marinade cool completely.

Season the fish with salt and pepper and arrange them in the marinade in a single layer. Refrigerate overnight.

The following day, peel the lemons with a sharp knife, making sure to remove all of the bitter white pith. Cut the lemons into wafer-thin slices and scatter them over the fish. Put the dish on the stove and bring the contents to a simmer. Simmer for 30 seconds and then remove the dish from the heat.

Carefully drain the marinade liquid into a small saucepan and bring to a boil. Then turn down the heat and simmer the marinade until it has reduced by one third, about 15 minutes. Pour this reduction over the fish. As the liquid cools, turn the fish from time to time. When completely cooled, refrigerate overnight or up to 2 days.

To serve, scatter the chervil leaves over the sardines. Accompany the marinated sardines with a sauceboat of fresh tomato sauce.

Terrine ménagère aux foies de volaille

Family-Style Chicken Liver Terrine

To serve 6:

1   pound chicken livers or a mixture of 12
    ounces chicken livers and 4 ounces chicken
    hearts

6   ounces fresh pork belly

6   ounces sausage meat

6   tablespoons armagnac or cognac

3   tablespoons red port

3   tablespoons sherry

1   tablespoon finely chopped garlic

⅔   cup chopped parsley

1   teaspoon thyme flowers or ½ teaspoon
thyme leaves

1   teaspoon sugar

Nutmeg

1¾   teaspoons salt

2   pinches pepper

½   pound barding fat, sliced thin

4   bay leaves

4   small sprigs thyme

Pickled onions and sour gherkins *(cornichons)*
as accompaniments

1-quart ovenproof terrine

Cut the livers and hearts in half. Cut the pork belly into slices ¾ inch
thick and then cut the slices crosswise into rectangular pieces about ½
inch wide. Put the pieces of pork, the chicken livers, and hearts in a
large bowl with the sausage meat. Add the armagnac, port, sherry,
garlic, parsley, thyme, sugar, a grating of nutmeg, salt, and pepper.
Mix together thoroughly, cover, and refrigerate overnight.

   Line the bottom and sides of the terrine with the slices of barding
fat, reserving some of the fat for covering the top of the terrine once it
has been filled. Stir all the ingredients that were marinated together
and pour them into the terrine. Completely cover the top with
the remaining barding fat and place the bay leaves and sprigs of thyme
on top.

   Preheat the oven to 425° F. Put the terrine in a high-sided roasting pan or baking dish and add enough water to the pan to come about halfway up the sides of the terrine. Put in the oven and bake for 1 hour and 45 minutes. The top will be a light-caramel color by the end of the cooking time. Remove the terrine from the oven and take it out of the pan of water. Let the terrine cool for 3 hours at room temperature and then refrigerate overnight before serving.

Serve the terrine as it is: Cut it into thin slices at the table and serve with *cornichons* and pickled onions.

Le foie de canard à la cuillère

Duck Liver Pâté

To serve 4 to 6:

½   pound fresh pork fat, cubed

¾   pound (about 1⅓ cups) duck livers, trimmed
     (see **NOTE***)*

2   teaspoons salt

½   teaspoon pepper

½   teaspoon *quatre épices (see page 211)*

1   cup *crème fraîche (page 206)*

4   egg yolks

2   tablespoons armagnac or cognac

A 1½-quart shallow baking dish

NOTE: *Duck livers are generally available at Chinese markets and may be found at specialty butchers and some supermarkets. Ed.*

Preheat the oven to 400° F.

In a food processor or an electric blender, purée the cubed pork fat until completely smooth. Add the duck livers, salt, pepper, and *quatre épices* and blend or process until the mixture is smooth and creamy. Then add the *crème fraîche,* egg yolks, and armagnac and whir until the mixture is thoroughly combined. Put a teaspoon of the mixture on a piece of aluminum foil and bake a few moments until firm. Taste and add more seasoning to the mixture if needed.

Strain the liver mixture into the shallow baking dish and cover the dish with aluminum foil. Set the dish in a baking pan somewhat larger than the dish and add enough water to the pan to come halfway up the side of the dish. Bake in the preheated oven about 35 minutes, until a knife inserted in the center of the pâté comes out clean.

Remove the pâté from the oven, let it cool completely, and then refrigerate overnight. Serve the pâté with toasted country-style bread.

Les entrées chaudes

WARM
APPETIZERS

Feuilletés de choux-fleurs et broccolis

Cauliflower and Broccoli in Puff Pastry

To serve 4:

Sixteen 1- to 1½-inch broccoli flowerets, stems removed

Sixteen 1- to 1½-inch cauliflower flowerets, stems removed

⅔ pound puff pastry *(page 207)* or buy the pastry *(page 212)*

SAUCE:

¼ cup of the vegetable cooking liquid, from above

3 tablespoons fresh chervil leaves *(see page 212 for substitution)*

¼ cup *crème fraîche (page 206)*

½ pound cold butter

Salt and pepper

1 tablespoon lemon juice

Bring salted water to a boil in a saucepan. Add the broccoli flowerets, return to a boil, and cook for 3 minutes. Remove them from the water, refresh them under cold running water, and then drain. Boil the cauliflower flowerets in the same water for 5 minutes and then refresh and drain them in the same way. Reserve ¼ cup of the cooking liquid, discard the rest, return the vegetables to the pan, and set them aside.

Preheat the oven to 425° F.

On a floured work surface, roll out the puff pastry to measure 10½ inches long, 6½ inches wide, and ¼ inch thick. Trim this to a rectangle 9½ inches long and 5½ inches wide. Cut this rectangle into 4 smaller rectangles of equal size. Turn the rectangles over and put them on a baking sheet. Bake them in the preheated oven until puffed and nicely browned, 25 to 30 minutes. Turn the oven off and keep the pastry warm in the cooling oven with the door ajar.

SAUCE:

Reheat the broccoli and cauliflower flowerets, uncovered, over very low heat. Put the reserved cooking liquid into a heavy-based saucepan. Add 2 tablespoons of the chervil leaves, bring to a boil, and continue boiling until the liquid is reduced by half, 2 to 3 minutes. Whisk in the *crème fraîche* and then the butter, a little bit at a time, so it softens and forms a sauce but does not melt completely. *(See page 199 for full instructions on how to make this type of sauce.)* Season the sauce with salt, pepper, and the lemon juice. Add the warm vegetables and turn the heat down as low as possible to keep barely warm.

Remove the pastry rectangles from the oven and, with a serrated knife, carefully cut each one in half horizontally. Put a bottom half on each of 4 individual plates or put them all on a serving platter. Arrange the flowerets on the pastries, alternating broccoli and cauliflower, spoon the sauce over them, and sprinkle with the remaining 1 tablespoon chervil leaves. Cover with the pastry tops and serve immediately.

Tarte fine à la tomate fraîche et au basilic

Fresh Tomato and Basil Tarts

To serve 4:

12	fresh basil leaves *(see page 211 for substitution)*
5	tablespoons olive oil
¾	pound puff pastry *(page 207)* or buy the pastry *(page 212)*
4	teaspoons tomato paste

4   medium-size ripe tomatoes, cored and sliced
⅛ inch thick

¼   teaspoon sugar

¼   teaspoon dried thyme

    Salt and pepper

Chop 6 of the basil leaves and macerate in 1 tablespoon of the olive oil.

Preheat the oven to 425° F.

With a rolling pin, roll the puff pastry out on a floured work surface to an 18-inch square that's as thin as possible, about ⅟₁₆ inch thick. Cut out four 8½-inch circles and transfer them to an oiled baking sheet. To prevent the pastry from rising during cooking, prick it thoroughly, every half inch or so, with the tines of a fork to within ½ inch of the edges.

Spread the olive oil and basil mixture and the tomato paste over the pastry circles, leaving a ½-inch rim. Cover with the tomato slices and sprinkle the sugar and thyme evenly over the tarts. Season with salt and pepper. Bake the tarts in the preheated oven for 25 to 30 minutes.

Halfway through the cooking time, remove the baking sheet from the oven. Remove the tarts and brush the baking sheet with some of the olive oil. Return the tarts to the sheet and brush the tops with olive oil. Put the tarts back in the oven to finish baking. When they are fully cooked, chop the remaining basil, sprinkle it over the tarts, and serve.

Tarte de tomates fraîches au thym minceur

Minceur Fresh Tomato and Spinach Tarts with Thyme

To serve 4:

20 large spinach leaves

1 quart cooked chopped fresh tomatoes *(page 205)*

Salt and pepper

4 small sprigs thyme or pinches dried thyme

4 individual ovenproof baking dishes or blini pans, about 5 inches in diameter

Preheat the oven to 425° F.

Cut off the stems of the spinach, blanch the leaves in boiling water for 2 minutes, and spread them out flat on a towel to drain. Line the baking dishes or blini pans with the spinach leaves; they must cover the bottom and sides, with extra overhang on the sides so that they can be folded back over the filling to completely enclose it.

Drain the tomatoes of excess liquid if necessary. Spoon them into the dishes and put the sprigs of thyme in the centers. Fold the spinach leaves over the top and bake the tarts in the preheated oven for 15 minutes. Serve in the baking dishes or pans.

Tourte aux oignons doux minceur

Minceur Onion Tart

To serve 4:

FILLING:

1   large carrot, cut into ¼-inch dice

1   teaspoon olive oil (optional)

1   pound mild onions, diced
    Salt and pepper

¼   pound mushrooms, cut into ¼-inch dice
    Pinch of thyme or thyme flowers

1   egg

¾   cup milk made with nonfat dry milk and
    water

8   or more leaves green cabbage, ribs trimmed
    off
    Fresh tomato sauce *(page 201),* artichoke
    sauce *(page 202),* or asparagus sauce *(page
    202)*

Baking dish about 7 inches in diameter and 1½ inches deep

FILLING:

In a saucepan, cook the carrot until it gives off its liquid, stirring often
to keep it from sticking. (The process is easier if you add the 1 teaspoon olive oil.) Cook for 5 minutes, then add the onions, and season
with salt and pepper. Cook together, covered, over low heat for 15
minutes, stir in the mushrooms and the thyme, and cook another 10
minutes. Drain off excess liquid if necessary.

In a bowl, beat the egg lightly with a fork to break it up. Add the
milk, season with salt and pepper, and mix. Add the cooked vegetables to the egg-and-milk mixture.

Blanch the cabbage leaves in boiling salted water for 4 minutes and spread them flat on a cloth to drain.

Preheat the oven to 425° F.

Line the baking dish with the cabbage leaves. They must cover the bottom and sides of the dish, with extra overhang on the sides so that the leaves can be folded back over the filling to completely enclose it.

Pour the filling into the baking dish, fold the cabbage leaves over the filling, and cover with aluminum foil. Set the baking dish in a somewhat larger pan and add enough water to the pan to come halfway up the sides of the dish. Carefully transfer to the preheated oven and bake for 50 minutes. Remove the tourte from the oven and let it stand for 10 to 15 minutes so that it will keep its shape when it is unmolded.

Before unmolding, tip off any excess liquid. Then unmold onto a platter. Pour the sauce you have chosen to use in a ribbon around the tourte.

Oeuf poché sur sa tomate grillée aux fines herbes

Baked Stuffed Tomatoes with Poached Eggs and Hollandaise

To serve 2 (see NOTE*):*

4 fresh spinach leaves

MUSHROOM STUFFING:

2   teaspoons olive oil

¼   pound mushrooms, finely chopped (about 1 cup)

3   garlic cloves, finely chopped

1   shallot, finely chopped

1   tablespoon chopped fresh chervil *(see page 212 for substitution)*

Salt and pepper

4   medium-size ripe tomatoes

Salt and pepper

2   tablespoons olive oil

Hollandaise sauce *(page 200)*, with 1
tablespoon chopped fresh chervil and ½
teaspoon chopped fresh tarragon *(see page
212 for substitutions)*

Vinegar (for acidulating the poaching water)

4   eggs

Bring a small saucepan of salted water to a boil and add the spinach
leaves. When the water returns to a boil, drain the spinach, refresh
under cold running water, and then spread the leaves on paper towels
to dry.

Preheat the oven to 400° F.

MUSHROOM STUFFING:

Heat the 2 teaspoons olive oil in a frying pan, add the chopped mushrooms, garlic, shallot, and chervil, and sauté quickly until softened.
Season with salt and pepper.

Cut off the tops of the tomatoes and reserve. With a small spoon
or with your fingers, scoop out and discard the seeds from the
tomatoes. Put the tomatoes in a baking dish and season them with salt
and pepper. Fill the tomatoes with the stuffing and replace the tops.
Baste the stuffed tomatoes with the 2 tablespoons olive oil and bake
them in the preheated oven for 10 minutes.

Meanwhile, make the hollandaise sauce, whisk in the fresh chervil
and tarragon, and keep the sauce warm. When the tomatoes have
baked for 10 minutes, turn the oven off and leave them in the oven,
with the door ajar, to keep warm.

Fill a shallow saucepan ¾ full of water and add about 3 tablespoons
vinegar per quart of water. Bring the acidulated water to a bare simmer. Break the eggs into the simmering water and poach them until
the whites are just set, about 4 minutes. With a slotted spoon, lift out

the eggs, transfer them to paper towels, and trim away any ragged edges.

Put the tomatoes on 2 individual plates. Remove the tops and nestle a poached egg in each tomato. Spoon some of the hollandaise sauce over the eggs and pour the remaining sauce into a sauceboat. Replace the tomato tops, garnish each plate with 2 spinach leaves, and serve immediately.

NOTE: *This is an instance—there are several in the book—in which Michel Guérard's generous portions may seem more than appropriate to you. We recommend one egg-topped tomato per person. Ed.*

Oeufs poule au caviar

Scrambled Eggs in Their Shells with Caviar

To serve 4:

8   eggs

2   teaspoons butter

1   tablespoon *crème fraîche (page 206)*

2   teaspoons finely chopped onion

2   teaspoons chopped chives

   Salt and pepper

4   ounces (8 tablespoons) caviar *(see* **NOTES***)*

12 long thin pieces of toasted bread or 12 cooked asparagus tips

8 egg cups

Using a serrated knife or a soft-boiled-egg cutter, cut all 8 eggshells about ½ inch down from their pointed ends. Empty 6 of the eggs into a bowl. (The remaining 2 eggs will not be needed; use them for something else.) Save the emptied shells, tops and bottoms, wash them carefully in warm water, and turn upside down on a towel to dry completely.

Melt the butter in a small saucepan over low heat and remove the pot from the heat. Beat the eggs lightly with a whisk and strain them through a sieve to eliminate all filaments. Pour the beaten eggs into the warm butter and put over very low heat. Beat constantly with the whisk until the eggs are thick and creamy but not solid. Remove the eggs immediately from the heat and continue whisking while adding the *crème fraîche,* onion, chives, and salt and pepper.

Place the dried eggshells in eggcups. Using an ordinary teaspoon, carefully fill each shell three-quarters full with the creamed eggs and then finish filling each shell with 1 tablespoon of caviar; the caviar should be slightly domed on top. Place the little top of each shell on the caviar. Serve the eggs with strips of toasted bread or warm asparagus tips, to be dipped into the egg and caviar and eaten with the fingers.

NOTES: These eggs can be served hot or cold. If served cold, the eggs should be cooked and the shells filled in advance, then chilled, but the caviar should be added at the last minute. The caviar can be replaced by an equal amount of either black or red lumpfish caviar. Thinly sliced pieces of either smoked salmon or eel could also be used instead of caviar.

Oeufs poule au caviar minceur

Minceur Scrambled Eggs in Their Shells

Make as the preceding recipe, but substitute 4 teaspoons *fromage blanc* (*page 206*) for the butter and *crème fraîche,* cut the amount of caviar in half, and serve without an accompaniment.

Cresson à l'oeuf poché

Watercress Purée with Poached Eggs

To serve 4:

Watercress purée *(page 145)*
Vinegar (for acidulating the poaching water)
4 eggs
8 fresh asparagus tips
4 slices truffle (optional)

Make the watercress purée but do not add the lemon juice and *crème fraîche* in the recipe yet.

Fill a shallow saucepan ¾ full of water and add about 3 tablespoons vinegar per quart of water. Bring the acidulated water to a bare simmer. Break the eggs into the simmering water and poach them until the whites are just set, about 4 minutes. With a slotted spoon, lift out the eggs, transfer them to paper towels, and trim away any ragged edges.

Cook the asparagus tips in boiling salted water for about 5 minutes and keep them warm. Reheat the watercress purée, add the lemon juice and *crème fraîche,* and spoon the purée onto 4 individual plates. Put one poached egg in the middle of the purée and decorate each with a slice of truffle on top and an asparagus tip on either side.

Crêpes soufflées au fromage

Cheese Soufflé Crêpes

To serve 4:

CRÊPES:

1   egg

1   egg yolk

⅔   cup flour

    Salt

¾   cup milk

1   tablespoon each chopped parsley and fresh tarragon (optional)

3   tablespoons butter

SOUFFLÉ MIXTURE:

¾   cup milk

1½ tablespoons butter

2½ tablespoons flour

    Salt and pepper

    Nutmeg

2   egg yolks

2   ounces gruyère cheese, grated (about ½ cup)

4   egg whites

8   thin slices cooked ham

2   tablespoons grated gruyère cheese

7-inch crêpe pan or small frying pan

CRÊPES:

In an electric blender, combine the whole egg, the egg yolk, the ⅔ cup flour, and pinch of salt. Add the ¾ cup milk, a little bit at a time, and blend until all of the milk has been added and the batter is smooth. Blend in the chopped herbs, if using. In the crêpe pan, melt the 3 tablespoons butter and cook it over medium heat until it is brown. Then add it to the batter and blend well. Let the batter rest for 30 minutes.

NOTE: *The crêpe batter can be made almost as easily by hand. Put the whole egg, the yolk, flour, salt, and half the milk in a mixing bowl and whisk until well combined. Whisk in the remaining milk, the herbs, and the brown butter. If the batter is at all lumpy, strain it. Ed.*

Brush the crêpe pan lightly with butter and set it over moderately high heat. When the pan is hot, pour in ⅛ of the batter and tilt and turn the pan to coat the bottom as thinly and evenly as possible. Cook the crêpe until the top looks dry and the edges begin to curl, about 10 seconds. Then turn the crêpe over with your fingers (the edges will be cool enough to handle) or with a spatula and cook the other side for about 8 seconds. Both sides should be lightly browned. Transfer the crêpe to a plate, and repeat this process with the remaining batter, piling the crêpes one on top of the other as you go. When all of the crêpes have been made, cover them with aluminum foil to keep them warm.

SOUFFLÉ MIXTURE:

Scald the milk. While the milk is heating, prepare the *roux*. In a small saucepan, melt the butter, whisk in the flour, and cook until bubbling but not browned, about 2 minutes. Pour on the scalded milk, whisk well, and continue to cook the mixture until it is smooth and fairly thick. Season it well with salt and pepper and grate in some nutmeg; it should be highly seasoned because egg whites, which will be added later, are very bland. Cook the mixture for 2 more minutes and then whisk in the 2 egg yolks. After 30 seconds, add the ½ cup grated cheese, whisk well, and remove the saucepan from the heat.

❨ NOTE: *The recipe can be prepared ahead to this point. Ed.*

Preheat the oven to 400° F.

Beat the egg whites until they are stiff. Reheat the soufflé mixture until it is hot to the touch. Fold ⅓ of the beaten egg whites into the soufflé mixture to lighten it. Then gently fold the mixture into the remaining egg whites.

Place a slice of ham on each crêpe. Spoon ⅛ of the soufflé mixture onto one half of each crêpe and fold the other half over it. Transfer the filled crêpes to a buttered ovenproof serving platter and sprinkle with the 2 tablespoons grated gruyère. Bake the crêpes in the preheated oven until the soufflé mixture has puffed, about 5 minutes. Serve immediately.

NOTE: The gruyère can be replaced by roquefort or parmesan cheese, and the crêpes can be replaced by blanched green cabbage leaves.

NOTE: *These are generous servings. You may find that 1 crêpe per person makes a nice first course. Serve 2 each as a luncheon dish. Ed.*

Mousseline de Saint-Jacques, sauce cressonnière

Scallop Mousselines with Watercress Sauce

To serve 4:

SAUCE:

1 bunch (about ½ pound) watercress, large stems removed

4 tablespoons cold butter

1 small shallot, chopped

⅓ cup chicken stock *(pages 194–195)*

¾ cup *crème fraîche (page 206)*

2 teaspoons lemon juice

   Salt and pepper

MOUSSELINES:

6 ounces scallops, with coral if available

   Salt and pepper

1 egg

1 cup *crème fraîche (page 206)*

Four 3½-inch ramekins or custard cups

SAUCE:

Bring a large pan of salted water to a boil. Set aside 8 sprigs of watercress and add the rest to the boiling water. When the water returns to a boil, drain the watercress and refresh it under cold running water. Squeeze the watercress to extract as much water as possible. Put it in a food processor or an electric blender and purée.

Melt 1 tablespoon of the butter in a medium-size saucepan, add the chopped shallot, and sauté it gently until soft. Add the chicken stock, bring to a boil, and continue boiling until it has reduced in volume by three-fourths—to about 1½ tablespoons. Stir in the ¾ cup *crème fraîche* and reduce the sauce by about one half—to a scant ½ cup. Add to the watercress in the processor or blender and whir. Strain the watercress mixture into a heavy-based saucepan and set aside.

MOUSSELINES:

Season the scallops well with salt and pepper and purée them in an electric blender or a food processor until very smooth, about 4 minutes. Add the egg and whir for 1 minute more. Put the container of the blender or processor in the refrigerator.

Butter the ramekins and preheat the oven to 425° F.

When the purée is well chilled, after about 30 minutes, add the 1 cup *crème fraîche,* and whir in the blender or processor until thoroughly blended. Taste for seasoning and add more if needed.

Pour the mousseline mixture into the ramekins and set them in a baking pan just large enough to hold them comfortably. Add enough water to the pan to come halfway up the sides of the ramekins and cover the pan with aluminum foil. Carefully transfer to the preheated oven and cook the ramekins until a knife inserted into a mousseline is clean when withdrawn, 30–40 minutes.

Shortly before the mousselines are done, finish the sauce. Heat the strained watercress mixture. Turn the heat down as low as possible and whisk in the remaining 3 tablespoons cold butter, a little bit at a time. *(See page 199 for complete instructions on making a sauce of this type.)* When all of the butter has been incorporated, stir in the lemon juice and season the sauce with salt and pepper to taste. Remove the saucepan from the heat.

When the mousselines are set, remove them from the water bath and dry the ramekins. Run a knife around the inside of each one and unmold the mousselines onto individual plates or a serving platter. Spoon the watercress sauce over the mousselines, garnish with the reserved watercress sprigs, and serve immediately.

NOTES: Almost any uncooked fish or shellfish can be substituted for the scallops used here. An equal weight of any shellfish, such as shrimp or lobster, could be directly substituted. Lean fish, such as pike, turbot, John Dory, whiting, sole, or hake fillets can be used, too. The procedure remains the same, but only ¼ pound of fillets is needed. A delicate variation of this recipe can be achieved by puréeing ¼ pound of any of the above-mentioned fish in a food processor or blender with 1 cup of milk, 1 egg, and 2 egg yolks. Cook this mixture as above. The result is meltingly tender and delicious. The watercress sauce used in this recipe can be replaced by fresh tomato sauce (*page 201*) flavored with chopped fresh tarragon or basil.

Huîtres au champagne minceur

Minceur Baked Oysters with Champagne

To serve 4:

24   shucked oysters with their liquor

Coarse salt or fine white gravel (to make a
bed for the oysters)

24   oyster half shells, the shallow halves if they
are deep enough to hold both oyster and
sauce, otherwise the deep halves, well rinsed

1   cup champagne or white wine

4   egg yolks

2   teaspoons *crème fraîche (page 206)*

Pepper

Preheat the oven to 475° F.

Through a cloth-lined sieve, filter the oyster liquor into a stainless
saucepan. Into a baking pan large enough to hold all the oysters in one
layer, pour coarse salt to a depth of about 1 inch and set the shells in
the salt. Warm the pan and shells over direct heat or, briefly, in the
hot oven.

In a heavy-based saucepan, boil the champagne until it is reduced
by three fourths, to about 2 tablespoons. Allow this to cool to luke-
warm and meanwhile separate the eggs and lightly whisk the yolks in
a bowl.

Off the heat, whisk into the reduced champagne first 2 teaspoons
cold water and the *crème fraîche* and then the egg yolks. Put the saucepan back over low heat and heat, whisking constantly, until the mixture thickens and becomes creamy. It must not heat past lukewarm
(test with your finger); it is thick enough when the movement of the
whisk exposes streaks of the bottom of the pan. Keep the sauce warm.

Bring the oyster liquor to a simmer, add the oysters, and poach
them, turning once, until the edges just begin to curl, about 30 sec-

onds. Drain, reserving the cooking liquor, and place each oyster in a half shell.

Whisk the hot oyster liquor bit by bit into the egg-yolk sauce, season with pepper, and spoon a little of the sauce over each oyster. Bake them in the preheated oven until the sauce is glazed and golden, about 30 seconds. Transfer the shells to individual soup plates and serve.

Escargots en pots aux croûtons

Snails in Pots with Toast

To serve 4:

SNAIL BUTTER:

½	pound butter, softened
6	large garlic cloves
2	cups, tightly packed parsley leaves
1	teaspoon Dijon mustard
2	tablespoons ground almonds (optional)
	Salt and pepper
	Nutmeg
½	cup diced ham
2	mushrooms, diced
½	cup cooked chopped fresh tomatoes *(page 205)*
48	snails, drained
8	slices homemade-type white bread
3½	tablespoons butter, softened

48 snail pots

SNAIL BUTTER:

Put the butter, garlic, parsley, mustard, almonds, salt and pepper, and a grating of nutmeg in a food processor or an electric blender and whir until combined. Transfer to a bowl and stir in the ham and mushrooms.

Divide the tomatoes among the snail pots, place a snail in each pot, and fill the pots with the snail butter.

Butter the slices of bread with the 3½ tablespoons butter and use a small cookie cutter or knife to cut out 48 rounds that are small enough to fit easily into the snail pots. Place the little pieces of bread, buttered side up, on top of the filled pots.

❑ NOTE: *The recipe can be made ahead to this point. Ed.*

Preheat the oven to 425° F.

Bake the snail pots in the oven for 10 minutes. The pieces of bread should have begun to brown and the snail butter should be hot and creamy but not completely melted when the snails are served.

Les escargots sans ail "Jacques Laffite"

Snails with Herb Cream Sauce

To serve 6:

3 cans (about 60) snails, drained, reserving ¾ cup of the liquid

SAUCE:

1 lemon

½ cup white wine

3 shallots, finely chopped

¾ cup reserved snail liquid, from above

6½ tablespoons *crème fraîche (page 206)*

½ pound cold butter

1 teaspoon each finely chopped fresh chervil, parsley, tarragon, and basil *(see pages 211–212 for substitutions)*

5 tablespoons chopped fresh tomatoes *(page 204)*

 Salt and pepper

CROÛTONS:

Twelve ½-inch-thick slices French bread (about 2½ inches in diameter)

⅓ cup olive oil

SAUCE:

Cut four ½-inch-wide strips of zest from the lemon. Cut them crosswise into very fine julienne strips. In a small saucepan of boiling water, blanch the zest for 5 minutes, drain, refresh under cold running water, and drain well.

In a heavy-based saucepan, bring the wine and the shallots to a boil and continue boiling until the wine has almost evaporated but the shallots are still moist, about 5 minutes. Add the reserved snail liquid and boil again as above until it has all but evaporated. Reduce the heat to the lowest point. Whisk in the *crème fraîche* and then the butter, a little bit at a time. *(See page 199 for full instructions on how to make this type of sauce.)* Stir in the herbs, the chopped tomato, and the julienned lemon zest. Add the snails. Season with salt, pepper, and lemon juice to taste. (**NOTE:** *You will probably use most, if not all, of the juice from the lemon. The lemon flavor should be noticeable but should not overwhelm the flavors of the other ingredients. Ed.)* While quickly making the croûtons, leave the snails and their sauce on the burner in order to warm the snails.

CROÛTONS:

Brush the slices of bread generously on both sides with the olive oil and toast under a broiler. The surfaces should be crisp and the interiors still slightly soft.

Spoon the snails and their sauce into 4 warmed, large but shallow bowls and arrange the croûtons around the edge of each serving.

NOTE: *To serve 4 we suggest 2 cans of snails, half the sauce, and 8 croûtons. Ed.*

Les salades

SALADS

Salade des prés à la ciboulette minceur

Minceur Fruit, Mushroom, and Chive Salad

To serve 4:

½ pound thin young green beans

1 small grapefruit

1 apple

¼ pound fresh or canned *cèpes* or fresh mushrooms

1 carrot, grated

2 tablespoons drained canned white ʻ'shoe-peg" corn kernels

½ cup vinaigrette minceur *(page 204)*

4 lettuce leaves

2 tablespoons chopped chives

Cook the green beans in boiling salted water until just tender, about 5 minutes. Refresh under cold running water and drain. Using a small knife and holding the grapefruit over a bowl to catch the juice, peel it completely down to the flesh. Cut the sections out from between the membranes and put the sections in the bowl with the juice. Peel and core the apple and cut it into thin half-moon slices. Mix the slices well with the grapefruit so they are coated with the juice.

If you have fresh *cèpes,* blanch them in boiling salted water for 1 minute, drain, and then cut into thin slices. Or, drain and slice the canned *cèpes.* Or, use fresh mushrooms thinly sliced and left raw.

Toss each of the vegetables—green beans, *cèpes* or mushrooms, grated carrot, canned corn—in separate bowls with enough vinaigrette to coat.

To serve, arrange lettuce leaves on 4 plates. Mound the green beans in the middle. Arrange the grapefruit sections, apple slices, *cèpes* or mushrooms, and grated carrot in a ring around the beans and sprinkle the corn kernels and chopped chives over all.

Salade de homard

Lobster Salad

To serve 4:

2 quarts court-bouillon *(pages 198–199)*

One 2-pound lobster

¾ pound green beans

24 fresh asparagus tips

MAYONNAISE:

2 egg yolks

1 teaspoon Dijon mustard

6 tablespoons olive oil

6 tablespoons peanut oil

Salt and pepper

2 teaspoons lemon juice

1 teaspoon tomato paste

1 teaspoon chopped fresh tarragon *(see page 212 for substitution)*

¼ teaspoon armagnac (optional)

1 small shallot, chopped

8 lettuce leaves

2 tablespoons fresh chervil leaves *(see page 212 for substitution)*

In a large pot, bring the court-bouillon to a boil, add the lobster, and boil rapidly for 10 minutes. Lift the lobster out of the pot and set aside to cool. Reserve the vegetables from the court-bouillon.

Detach the tail of the lobster, then cut the rings on the underside with large scissors, and remove the meat. Cut the tail meat into 8 slices. Crack the claws with a nutcracker or by hitting them with the blunt edge of a cleaver, remove the meat, and cut each piece in half lengthwise.

Cook the green beans in boiling salted water until just tender, 5 to 8 minutes. Lift out with a slotted spoon, refresh under cold running water, drain, and set aside in a small bowl.

Cook the asparagus tips in the same water until just tender. Refresh, drain, and set aside in a separate bowl.

MAYONNAISE:

In a bowl, whisk together the egg yolks and mustard. Whisk in the oils, a few drops at a time, and season with salt and pepper and lemon juice. Add the tomato paste, tarragon, armagnac, and 1 heaping tablespoon of the vegetables from the court-bouillon. This sauce will be more liquid than an ordinary mayonnaise.

Pour ¼ of the mayonnaise over the beans and ¼ over the asparagus. Sprinkle each with ½ the chopped shallot and toss.

Place 2 lettuce leaves on each plate. Make a mound of beans in the center of each plate, stick the asparagus tips here and there in the mound of beans, and scatter the chervil leaves over the top. Arrange the slices of lobster tail around the beans and pour the remaining mayonnaise over the lobster. Stick a piece of claw meat in the center of each mound of beans, the pointed end sticking up, and serve.

NOTES: For a less expensive salad, use mussels rather than lobster. A simple vinaigrette, seasoned with chopped fresh tarragon, is also very nice as a sauce for this salad.

Salade de poissons crus marinés minceur

Minceur Marinated Raw Fish Salad

To serve 4:

5 to 6	ounces firm-fleshed raw fish fillets—one or more kinds, such as salmon and bass
1	tablespoon olive oil
	Salt and pepper
½	shallot, finely chopped
2	teaspoons drained green peppercorns
1	lemon
1	head tender green lettuce, such as Bibb
1½	ounces ginger preserved in vinegar *(see* **NOTES**), cut into fine shreds
	A spoonful fresh huckleberries *(see* **NOTES**)

NOTES: *Ginger preserved in vinegar is available in Japanese grocery stores. It's called* beni shoga. *Michel Guérard's recipe calls for fresh* airelles, *or* bilberries, *which are close relatives of* myrtilles *in turn, approximately the equivalent of huckleberries. Wild blueberries would be delicious, or you could also use a spoonful of the smaller berries from a basket of cultivated blueberries, though these will be sweeter and less flavorful than the berries intended. Ed.*

With a thin sharp knife, cut the fish into slices so thin they are almost transparent. *(This is done horizontally, at only a slight slant, the way smoked salmon is cut. Ed.)* Spread the slices on a plate, drizzle the oil over them, and sprinkle them evenly with a little salt and pepper, the chopped shallot, and the green peppercorns.

Cut the zest from the lemon in thin strips and cut these into julienne strips as fine as pine needles. Blanch them in boiling water for 1 minute, drain, and refresh under cold running water. Wash and dry the lettuce and cut the leaves into strips ½ inch wide. In a bowl, toss the lettuce with lemon juice and salt and pepper to taste.

Make a bed of lettuce on each of 4 plates. Scatter over these the julienne strips of lemon zest and shredded ginger and the berries. Then arrange the slices of marinated fish on top, radiating from the centers like petals of flowers. Chill the salads in the refrigerator for at least 15 minutes before serving.

Salade gourmande

Asparagus and String Bean Salad with Foie Gras

To serve 4:

1	pound thin young green beans
24	thin young asparagus stalks, tough ends removed
8	tender lettuce leaves *(see* **NOTE***)*
¼	cup vinaigrette gourmande *(page 203)*
¼	pound *foie gras*
1½	ounces truffles, cut in fine julienne strips

NOTE: *Michel Guérard uses a red lettuce called* batavia *which we do not have in our markets. Small red oakleaf lettuce leaves are not as flavorful but good nevertheless. Ed.*

Bring a saucepan of salted water to a boil. Add the beans and cook them until just tender, about 5 minutes. Remove them from the pan with a slotted spoon, refresh them under cold running water, and drain them well. Cook the asparagus in the same water until just tender, about 5 minutes. Drain the asparagus, refresh, and drain well.

Arrange 2 lettuce leaves on each plate. Toss the beans and the asparagus in the vinaigrette and mound them in the center of the leaves. Dip the blade of a small paring knife into hot water and use it to shave thin slices of the *foie gras* over the mounded vegetables. Sprinkle the truffle julienne over the salads and serve.

Salade de jambon des Landes

Raw Ham, Pea, and Onion Salad

To serve 4:

1	head tender lettuce, such as Bibb
16	pearl onions *(see* **NOTES***)*
1½	cups fresh or frozen tiny green peas
½	cup vinaigrette gourmande *(page 203)*
1	pound raw ham, such as prosciutto, thinly sliced *(see* **NOTES***)*
	Pepper

NOTES: *If pearl onions aren't available, use green onions with their leaves cut off. The cooking time will be the same, but, of course, they needn't be blanched and peeled. We have no counterpart to* jambon des Landes. *Prosciutto is quite different, but it works well in this salad. Ed.*

Set aside 4 cupped lettuce leaves. Bring a saucepan of salted water to a boil, add the remaining lettuce leaves, and cook them for 4 minutes. Remove them with a slotted spoon, drain, and transfer to paper towels to dry. In the same water, blanch the onions for 10 seconds to loosen the peelings and then peel them. If using frozen peas, return the onions to the saucepan of boiling water and, after 1 minute, add the peas. Cook the vegetables together for 6 minutes. For fresh peas, cook 8 minutes, add the onions, and continue cooking 7 more minutes. Drain the vegetables well.

❡ **NOTE:** *The recipe can be prepared ahead to this point. Ed.*

Toss the onions, peas, and the cooked lettuce leaves with the vinaigrette. Put one of the reserved lettuce leaves on each plate and fill with the tossed salad. Surround each salad with slices of ham, grind pepper over the ham slices, and serve.

La salade grande ferme au saucisson chaud

Chicory with Warm Sausage and Potato Salad

To serve 4:

½ pound smoked sausage

½ pound small new potatoes

2 tablespoons vinegar

2 tablespoons white wine

1 shallot, finely chopped

2 tablespoons chopped parsley

GARLIC CROÛTONS:

Sixteen ½-inch-thick slices French bread (about 2½ inches in diameter)

5 tablespoons butter, softened

2 garlic cloves

⅓ pound slab bacon

1 head chicory

½ cup vinaigrette gourmande *(page 203)*

3 ounces roquefort cheese, crumbled (about ½ cup)

Bring a saucepan of water to a boil, add the sausage, reduce the heat, and simmer for 45 minutes. Put the potatoes in a pan of salted water, bring to a boil, reduce heat to moderate, and cook, uncovered, until tender, about 25 minutes.

Preheat the oven to 200° F.

When the potatoes and the sausage are cool enough to handle, peel them and cut them into slices ¼ inch thick. Spread out the slices in a baking pan and sprinkle with the vinegar, white wine, shallot, and 1 tablespoon of the chopped parsley. Put the dish in the preheated oven while you prepare the rest of the salad.

GARLIC CROÛTONS:

Butter both sides of the bread slices with the softened butter. In a large frying pan, brown on both sides as many of the slices as will fit in a single layer. Remove them from the frying pan and repeat until all of the slices have been browned. Rub the croûtons with the garlic, put them into a baking pan, and keep them warm in the oven.

Cut the bacon into ¼-inch slices and then cut the slices crosswise into ¼-inch *lardons*. In the frying pan, sauté the *lardons* until browned. Drain them on paper towels.

Separate the head of chicory. Toss the leaves with the vinaigrette. Add the warm garlic croûtons, the *lardons,* and the roquefort to the salad and toss again.

On a large serving plate, mound the tossed salad into a dome. Alternate the sausage and potato slices, forming a ring around the base of the dome. Sprinkle with the remaining parsley and serve.

Salade de lentilles aux croûtons d'anchoïde

Lentil Salad with Anchovy Croûtons

To serve 4:

1 cup lentils
Salt and pepper
Bouquet garni
½ onion, chopped
1 carrot, chopped
½ garlic clove, chopped

ANCHOVY CROÛTONS:

8 anchovy fillets
1 egg yolk
6 tablespoons olive oil
Twelve ½-inch-thick slices French bread (about 2½ inches in diameter)

DRESSING:

4 tablespoons peanut oil
4 tablespoons wine vinegar
1 small shallot, finely chopped
Salt and pepper

1 tablespoon chopped capers

Rinse the lentils and put them in a saucepan with water to cover. Bring to a boil, skim off any foam that rises to the surface, and add salt and pepper, the bouquet garni, onion, carrot, and garlic. Lower the heat, cover the pot, and simmer until the lentils are tender but not falling apart, about 35 minutes. Drain the lentils, remove the bouquet garni, and chill.

ANCHOVY CROÛTONS:

Put the anchovy fillets and the egg yolk in a food processor or an electric blender. Whir for 30 seconds and then add 4 tablespoons of the olive oil, 1 tablespoon at a time.

Brush both sides of each slice of bread with the remaining olive oil. Brown on both sides under the broiler and then spread one side of each croûton with a generous layer of the anchovy mixture.

DRESSING:

Whisk the peanut oil, vinegar, shallot, and a little salt and pepper together in a large bowl.

Add the lentils to the bowl and the capers and mix thoroughly with the dressing. Form the lentils into a dome, arrange the anchovy croûtons around the dome, and serve.

NOTES: A slice of tomato topped by a slice of hard-cooked egg and an anchovy fillet can be placed on each croûton instead of the anchovy paste described above. In this case, simply serve the croûtons on a plate along with the salad. To make this salad more colorful, white beans, soaked overnight and cooked for about 2 hours, can be substituted for half the lentils.

Salade de pommes de terre

Warm Potato Salad

To serve 4:

1¼   pounds small new potatoes

VINAIGRETTE:

1½   tablespoons white-wine vinegar

Salt and pepper

1   tablespoon juice drained from a can of truffles (*see* **NOTE**)

3   tablespoons white wine

3   tablespoons peanut oil

1   tablespoon chopped chives

1   shallot, chopped

Put the potatoes in a large pan of salted water, bring to a boil, reduce heat to moderate, and cook, uncovered, until tender, about 25 minutes.

VINAIGRETTE:

Whisk together the vinegar and salt and pepper. Add the truffle juice and wine and whisk in the oil, a little at a time. Stir in the chives and shallot. Taste and correct seasoning if necessary.

When the potatoes are just cool enough to handle, peel them and slice them into ¼-inch rounds. Transfer the slices to a bowl, add the prepared vinaigrette, and toss gently. Cover to keep the salad slightly warm until ready to serve.

NOTE: *Although the salad will lose some of its distinction, the truffle juice can be replaced by stock or by mushroom broth. With or without the truffle juice, it's an excellent accompaniment to grilled sausages or cold roast beef. Ed.*

Les crustacés, coquillages
& poissons

SHELLFISH
& FISH

Homard, langouste, ou écrevisses à la nage

Lobster, Spiny Lobster, or Crayfish in Court-Bouillon

To serve 4:

3 quarts court-bouillon *(pages 198–199)*
Two 1½- to 1¾-pound lobster or 20 crayfish
Chopped parsley (for garnish)

Bring the court-bouillon to a boil in a large pot, plunge in the lobster or crayfish and, as soon as the liquid returns to a simmer, time the cooking—12 minutes for lobsters and 2 minutes for crayfish. (**NOTE:** *Some American crayfish are larger than the European; they may need longer cooking. Ed.*) Remove the shellfish, strain the court-bouillon, and re-serve both it and its vegetables.

To serve lobster: Split it completely in half lengthwise, cutting from the bottom side. Remove and shell the claws. Remove the gritty sac in the back of the head. Arrange the lobster halves and the claw meat in a deep platter, top them with a generous spoonful of the vegetables, add a cup of the hot court-bouillon, and sprinkle with the chopped parsley.

To serve crayfish: Mound the whole crayfish in a pyramid in a large bowl, pour in a cup of the court-bouillon, and decorate with sprigs of parsley.

NOTES: The vein in the crayfish can be cleaned by keeping the live crayfish for 12 hours in cold water to which nonfat dry milk has been added. It is very important never to overcook lobster or crayfish, as this toughens them; they will be better even slightly undercooked. They should be allowed to rest for a few minutes after cooking and before serving. This "relaxes" the meat, which makes it even more tender.

Coquilles Saint-Jacques sautées au vermouth

Sautéed Scallops with Vermouth

To serve 4:

1   tablespoon butter

1   tablespoon olive oil

20   (about 1½ pounds) sea scallops *(see* NOTE*)*

SAUCE:

2   small shallots, finely chopped

¼   cup white wine

¼   cup vermouth

¼   cup chicken stock *(pages 194–195)*

2   cups heavy cream

2   tablespoons cold butter

Pinch saffron

½   cup cooked chopped fresh tomatoes *(page 205)*

Salt and pepper

1   tablespoon fresh chervil leaves

4 scallop shells for serving

Preheat the oven to 200° F.

In a large frying pan, combine the butter and olive oil and cook over medium heat until they are nut brown in color. Then add the scallops and sauté them for 3 minutes. With a slotted spoon, transfer the scallops to an ovenproof dish and keep them warm in the preheated oven. Put the scallop shells into the oven to warm them.

SAUCE:

Add the chopped shallots to the frying pan and sauté them for 1 minute. Pour in the white wine, vermouth, and chicken stock, increase the heat to high, and cook until the liquid has reduced to about ¼ cup. Then add the cream and reduce the combined liquids by half. Turn the heat down to very low and whisk in the cold butter, a little bit at a time. *(For full instructions on how to make this type of sauce, see page 199.)* Add the saffron, stir in the cooked tomatoes, and season with salt and pepper.

Divide the sautéed scallops among the heated shells. Spoon the sauce over the scallops, scatter the chervil leaves over all, and serve.

NOTE: *To substitute bay scallops, use the same weight but reduce the sautéing time to 1 minute. Ed.*

Coquilles Saint-Jacques à l'effilochée d'endives

Scallops with Endive Sauce

To serve 4:

ENDIVE SAUCE:

4	medium endives (about ½ pound in all)
2½	tablespoons butter
	Salt and pepper
1	teaspoon sugar
2	cups heavy cream
20	(about 1½ pounds) sea scallops *(see* **NOTE***)*
	Salt and pepper
¼	cup flour
4	tablespoons butter
1	generous tablespoon chopped fresh chervil *(see page 212 for substitution)*

ENDIVE SAUCE:

Cut the endives into julienne strips about ⅛ inch by 1½ inches. In a saucepan over medium heat, melt the 2½ tablespoons butter. When it stops sizzling and begins to turn light brown, add the endive. Sprinkle with salt and pepper and the sugar, brown the endive lightly, stirring frequently, and then cover and cook over low heat for 15 minutes. At the end of this time, add the cream and boil gently, uncovered, until the sauce thickens lightly, about 10 minutes.

Season the scallops with salt and pepper and coat lightly with flour. In a frying pan, melt the 4 tablespoons butter over high heat until it stops sizzling and begins to turn brown. Add the scallops and sauté them for 3 minutes. They should be lightly browned.

Divide the endive sauce among 4 plates or pour it onto a serving platter. Lift the scallops out of the frying pan and set them on the sauce. Sprinkle with the chervil and serve.

NOTES: To save time when making the sauce, you may simply cut the endives into very thin rounds rather than into julienne strips. This sauce is also delicious served with sautéed scallops of veal or with poached poultry.

NOTE: *To substitute bay scallops, use the same weight but reduce the sautéing time to 1 minute. Ed.*

Filets de limande sauce simple

Lemon Sole with Fresh Herb Sauce

To serve 4:

8   small (1½ to 2 pounds) lemon sole fillets *(see* **NOTE***)*
    Salt and pepper

FRESH HERB SAUCE:

3   tablespoons olive oil

1   small garlic clove, finely chopped

1   shallot, finely chopped

⅓   cup chopped fresh tomatoes *(page 204)*

    Pinch thyme

¼   bay leaf, crumbled

1   teaspoon each finely chopped chives and
    Italian flat-leaf parsley

½   teaspoon each finely chopped fresh tarragon
    and basil *(see pages 211–212 for substitutions)*

⅔   cup chicken stock *(pages 194–195)*

    Salt and pepper

6   tablespoons cold butter

2   tablespoons white wine

½   teaspoon lemon juice

6   tablespoons flour

3   tablespoons butter

1   tablespoon olive oil

1   tablespoon fresh chervil leaves *(see page 212
    for substitution)*

NOTE: *Any small sole or flounder fillets can be substituted for the lemon sole. Ed.*

Put the fillets between 2 pieces of parchment or waxed paper and flatten them a bit by pounding them lightly with a rolling pin. Season both sides of the fillets with salt and pepper.

FRESH HERB SAUCE:

Heat the olive oil in a heavy-based saucepan set over medium heat. Add the chopped garlic and shallot and cook until the vegetables are soft but not browned, about 2 minutes. Add the chopped tomato, thyme, and bay leaf and cook for 3 minutes. Then add all of the finely chopped fresh herbs and the chicken stock, season with salt and pepper, and simmer the mixture for 5 minutes. Whisk in the cold butter, a little bit at a time. *(See page 199 for full instructions on how to make this type of sauce.)* When the butter has been incorporated, add the white wine and the lemon juice. Whisk well and correct the seasoning. Remove the saucepan from the heat.

Coat the fish fillets lightly with flour. In a frying pan, heat the butter and olive oil until hot, add as many of the floured fillets as will fit in a single layer, and sauté them for 3 minutes on each side. Repeat with any remaining fillets.

Cover the bottom of 4 plates or a serving platter with the sauce. Arrange the sautéed fillets on the sauce and garnish with the fresh chervil leaves.

Truite en papillote à l'aneth et au citron minceur

Minceur Baked Trout with Dill and Lemon

To serve 4:

1	lemon
4	small (about ½ pound each) fresh or frozen trout, dressed
	Salt and pepper
4	sprigs fresh dill
1	shallot, finely chopped
1	tablespoon pale dry sherry
¼	cup fish stock *(pages 196–197)*
2	teaspoons olive oil

Four 12-inch rounds aluminum foil

Preheat the oven to 450° F.

With a small knife, peel the lemon completely, down to the flesh, and then cut in thin slices.

Set a fish on one half of each foil round and turn the edges up so you won't lose any liquid. Season the cavities of the fish with salt and pepper and put a sprig of dill in each one. Sprinkle the fish with the shallot, pour ¾ teaspoon of sherry, 1 tablespoon of fish stock, and ½ teaspoon of olive oil over each one, and cover them with the slices of lemon. Fold the loose half of the foil over each fish. Then fold and double-fold the edges of foil to make well-sealed turnover-like packages.

❦ **NOTE:** *The recipe can be prepared ahead to this point. Ed.*

Bake the trout in the preheated oven for 8 minutes. Remove the packages from the oven, put them on individual plates, and serve immediately. The diners open their own packages so that they can enjoy the concentrated aroma of the first burst of steam.

Carrelet au cidre

Flatfish Baked in Cider

To serve 2:

2	mushrooms
	Salt and pepper
1½	teaspoons nonfat dry milk
	Nutmeg
1	small apple
2	tablespoons lemon juice
	One 1½-pound flatfish, dressed *(see **NOTES**)*

½   cup fish stock *(pages 196–197)*

½   cup cider *(see* **NOTES***)*

½   shallot, finely chopped

1   teaspoon chopped fresh tarragon *(see page 212 for substitution)*

1   tablespoon chopped fresh tomato *(page 204)*

NOTES: *A carrelet is a flat, white-fleshed fish for which grey or lemon sole, flounder, hake, or plaice can be substituted. Fish larger than the weight specified can, of course, be cooked in this way to serve more people, with a longer cooking time as needed until the flesh can be easily pierced with a fork. The cider should be dry—not the sweet cider commonly found in the United States. You could use a dry hard cider or substitute white wine. Ed.*

Cut the mushrooms in half and put them in a small saucepan with 2 tablespoons water, the dry milk, salt and pepper, and a grating of nutmeg. Cook over low heat, uncovered, for 15 minutes. Purée the mushrooms along with a teaspoon of their cooking liquid in a blender. You should have about 1 tablespoon of purée.

Preheat the oven to 425° F.

Peel and core the apple and cut it into fine strips about ⅛ inch wide and 1½ inches long. Toss with the lemon juice.

Salt and pepper the fish. Combine the fish stock, cider, and mushroom purée. Sprinkle a baking dish with the shallot and tarragon, put in the fish, and pour in the stock-cider-mushroom mixture. Bake in the preheated oven, uncovered, basting 2 or 3 times with the cooking liquid in the dish, until the flesh can be easily pierced with a fork, 15 to 20 minutes. Halfway through the cooking time, spread the apples over the fish.

When it is done, remove the fish, skin it, and lift off the fillets. Place them on individual plates. Top with the apples and a little of the cooking liquid to moisten, scatter the chopped tomato over all, and serve.

Dos de colin rôti au four

Roast Hake or Haddock

To serve 4:

One 5-pound haddock, dressed *(see NOTE)*

2 large bay leaves, quartered

Salt and pepper

¼ cup olive oil

6 garlic cloves, unpeeled

2 ripe tomatoes, cut into sixths

2 cups chicken stock *(pages 194–195)*

4 tablespoons butter

NOTE: *We have used haddock rather than hake, as it is readily available and we found only small hake, considerably smaller than 5 pounds. Ed.*

Preheat the oven to 375° F.

Cut off the head and the narrow tail section of the fish and reserve for making fish stock. This center cut should weigh about 3 pounds and resemble a roast. With the tip of a sharp knife, make 8 small incisions along the back of the fish. Slip a piece of bay leaf into each cut. Season the inside of the fish with salt and pepper.

Pour the olive oil into a roasting pan and add the garlic cloves. Put the pan into the preheated oven for 5 minutes so the garlic flavors the oil. Then put the fish into the pan and roast it for 20 minutes, basting it with the seasoned oil every 5 minutes. After 10 minutes, add the tomatoes to the pan. Transfer the fish to an ovenproof platter, cover it tightly with aluminum foil, and put it back in the turned-off oven while you prepare the sauce.

Pour the chicken stock into the roasting pan and whisk well to dislodge any coagulated juices adhering to the bottom. Strain the liquid into a saucepan and press down on the garlic and tomatoes to extract all their juices. Cook the sauce until it has reduced by one third, about 15 minutes. Remove from the heat and whisk in the butter, a little bit at a time, to enrich the sauce and thicken it slightly. Season with salt and pepper and pour into a sauceboat.

Carve the fish roast and serve.

NOTE: Noodles in lemon sauce (*page 162*) are a particularly delicious accompaniment to this roast fish.

Poisson en baudrouche

Baked Red Snapper

To serve 4:

	One 2½-pound red snapper, dressed
	Salt and pepper
½	carrot, thinly sliced
1	small boiling onion, thinly sliced
1	leek, white part only, well washed and thinly sliced
½	lemon, peeled and cut into 4 slices
6	fresh tarragon leaves (*see page 212 for substitution*)
2	tablespoons fresh chervil leaves (*see page 212 for substitution*)
1	cup chicken stock (*pages 194–195*)
1	cup simple court-bouillon (*page 199*)
1	tablespoon vermouth
	Zest of 2 lemons, cut in fine julienne strips
1	tablespoon *crème fraîche (page 206)*
6	ounces cold butter
2	tablespoons chopped fresh herbs

Preheat the oven to 425° F.

Line a large baking dish loosely and generously with aluminum foil and lay the fish in the dish diagonally. Season it with salt and pepper. Scatter the sliced carrot, onion, leek, lemon, tarragon, and chervil over the fish. Pour the chicken stock, court-bouillon, and vermouth around the fish. Gather the edges of aluminum foil together and fold securely to completely enclose the fish and its cooking liquid in a foil package. Bake the fish in the preheated oven for 35 minutes.

While the fish is baking, bring a small saucepan of water to a boil. Add the julienned lemon zest, blanch it for 5 minutes, drain, rinse under cold running water, and drain well.

When the fish is done, remove it from the oven and carefully open the aluminum foil. Transfer the vegetables and ¾ cup of the cooking liquid to a small saucepan and bring to a boil. Whisk in the *crème fraîche*. Then turn the heat down as low as possible and whisk in the butter, a little bit at a time. *(See page 199 for complete instructions on making this type of sauce.)* Stir in the blanched lemon zest and season with salt and pepper. Turn off the heat.

Carefully skin the fish, remove the fillets, and transfer them to a warmed serving platter. Spoon some of the sauce over the fillets and sprinkle with the chopped fresh herbs. Pass the remaining sauce separately in a sauceboat.

NOTE: *The original of this recipe was for fish baked inside a large sausage casing. If you'd like to try this, make the recipe as described except put the fish and other ingredients into a length of casing and tie both ends, rather than wrapping them in foil. Though this simpler foil version may deprive the dish of some of its novelty, it is equally delicious. Ed.*

Steaks de lotte au poivre vert

Sautéed Monkfish with Green Peppercorns

To serve 4:

1⅓ pounds boneless monkfish, cut in 4 pieces

Salt and pepper

2 tablespoons flour

2 tablespoons olive oil

2 tablespoons butter

SAUCE:

3 tablespoons white wine

½ cup fish stock *(pages 196–197)*

1 teaspoon meat glaze *(see **NOTE**)*

¼ cup *crème fraîche (page 206)*

6 ounces cold butter

4 teaspoons drained green peppercorns

Salt and pepper

NOTE: *Meat glaze* (glace de viande) *can be purchased in jars at specialty food shops. It keeps forever and is wonderfully handy as its deep flavor lifts many dishes from so-so to superb. To make your own, cook homemade veal or beef stock all the way down to a syrupy glaze, about ¹⁄₁₀ of its original volume. There's really no trick to it, though you must turn the heat to a simmer and watch during the final stages of reduction so it doesn't burn, and you must begin with unsalted or very lightly salted stock, or the glaze will be too salty to use. Ed.*

Season the fish with salt and coat very lightly with flour. Heat the oil and butter in a frying pan over moderate heat, add the fish, and sauté it until just done, about 5 minutes on each side. Remove the fish from the pan and keep it warm.

SAUCE:

Pour any excess oil and butter out of the pan, stir in the white wine, and let it reduce by one fourth. Then add the fish stock, meat glaze, and *crème fraîche* and let cook until reduced by one half. Turn down to the lowest possible heat and whisk in the cold butter, a little bit at a time. *(See page 199 for full instructions on making this type of sauce.)* Stir in the green peppercorns and season the sauce with salt and pepper if needed.

Put the fish on individual plates, pour the sauce over the fish, and serve.

Poisson sur son compotée de tomates

Baked Cod with Tomatoes and Tomato Sauce

To serve 4:

2½ pounds ripe tomatoes
½ teaspoon drained green peppercorns
   Pinch dried basil
1½ tablespoons olive oil
   Salt and pepper
1½ pounds cod fillets, with the skin intact

SAUCE:
   Juice and peelings from tomatoes, above
2 tablespoons olive oil
   Pinch dried basil
   Salt and pepper

2   tablespoons butter

1   tablespoon fresh chervil leaves *(see page 212 for substitution)*

Preheat the oven to 350° F.

Core the tomatoes and cut them in half horizontally. With a small spoon or your fingers, scoop the tomato seeds and juice into a small saucepan and set aside. Put a rack on a baking sheet and set the halved tomatoes, cut side up, on the rack. Bake the tomatoes in the preheated oven for 20 minutes.

When the tomatoes are cool enough to handle, peel them and add the peelings to the reserved saucepan of juice. Put the tomatoes into a medium-size saucepan, add the peppercorns, basil, and olive oil, and season with salt and pepper. Stir with a whisk to blend in the seasonings and break up the tomatoes. *(**NOTE:** If the tomatoes are very juicy, quickly boil off the excess liquid over high heat but don't take this so far that the tomatoes are reduced to a sauce. Ed.)*

Set the saucepan of tomato juice and peelings over low heat and cook for 15 minutes. Strain out and discard the seeds and peelings and return the juice to the saucepan.

❡ **NOTE:** *The recipe can be prepared ahead to this point. Ed.*

Put the cod fillets in an oiled baking pan, season with salt and pepper, and either bake in a preheated 400° F. oven or broil, about 10 minutes in either case, until just cooked.

SAUCE:

While the fish is cooking, warm the tomato-peppercorn mixture over low heat. Bring the tomato juice to a boil. Whisk in the 2 tablespoons of olive oil and the basil and season with salt and pepper. Whisk the 2 tablespoons of butter into the sauce, a little bit at a time, and remove the pan from the heat.

Spoon a bed of the tomato-peppercorn mixture on each of 4 plates. Put the cod fillets on top of the tomatoes and pour a band of the tomato sauce around each serving. Scatter the chervil leaves over the fish and serve.

Dorade en croûte de sel

Porgy Baked in Salt

To serve 2:

3¼ pounds coarse salt

One 1¾-pound porgy, dressed but not scaled *(see* **NOTES***)*

Salt and pepper

½ cup fresh tomato sauce *(page 201)*

Sautéed leeks with cream *(page 153)*

Preheat the oven to 475° F.

Spread a third of the coarse salt evenly over the bottom of a deep baking dish just large enough to hold the fish. Lay the fish on top of the bed of salt and cover it with the remaining salt. Bake in the pre-heated oven for 30 minutes.

Remove the fish from the oven and show it to your guest as it is in the baking dish and then take it back to the kitchen to serve. Break the hardened crust of salt and lift it off of the fish. Remove the skin; because of the scales, it will lift off easily. With a long sharp knife, lift off the fillets from the bone and place them either on individual plates or on a serving platter. Salt the fillets very lightly if you think it necessary and sprinkle them with pepper.

Spoon the sauce over the fillets, spoon the sautéed leeks around the fillets, and serve immediately.

NOTES: As it cooks and hardens, the salt forms a hermetic "second oven" around the fish. The presentation of the fish in the salt always surprises people. Almost any saltwater fish can be cooked in this way—hake, haddock, cod, to name only a few. It is also an excellent way to cook fresh sardines and has a particular advantage in that case—the thick layer of salt keeps their strong odor from invading your kitchen.

Dorade cuite sur litière

Baked Porgy

To serve 2:

1   teaspoon olive oil (optional)

½   carrot, cut into ¼-inch dice

½   leek, white part only, well washed and cut into ¼-inch dice

½   onion, cut into ¼-inch dice

2   mushrooms, cut into ¼-inch dice

½   teaspoon chopped shallot

½   garlic clove, finely chopped

Sprig thyme

½   bay leaf

⅓   cup chopped fresh tomatoes *(page 204)*

6   tablespoons fish stock *(pages 196–197)*

One 1¾-pound porgy, dressed *(see* **NOTE***)*

1   teaspoon *crème fraîche (page 206)*

Salt and pepper

1   tablespoon chopped parsley

NOTE: *Any lean, white-fleshed flatfish could be used in this recipe. Ed.*

Preheat the oven to 425° F.

Heat a nonstick frying pan and add the carrot, leek, onion, mushrooms, shallot, garlic, thyme, and bay leaf. Cook the vegetables gently so they render their liquid, stirring occasionally. They should remain crisp-tender. (Or, you can heat the olive oil in a baking dish and cook the vegetables in it on top of the stove.)

Spread the vegetables in a baking dish and add the tomatoes and the fish stock. Place the fish on top and bake it in the preheated oven, basting it 3 or 4 times with the juices in the dish as it cooks, until the flesh can be pierced easily with a fork, 15 to 20 minutes. Remove the fish to a warm platter and keep it warm. Leave the oven on.

Strain the cooking liquid into a saucepan, discard the thyme and bay leaf, and reserve the vegetables. Boil the liquid over high heat to reduce it by one fourth, add the *crème fraîche,* and taste for seasoning.

Meanwhile, skin the fish and return it to the baking dish. Spread the vegetables over it and add the reduced cooking liquid. Return the fish to the hot oven for a few seconds to reheat, sprinkle with the parsley, and serve from the baking dish.

Dorade au beurre de piments doux

Porgy with Green Pepper Sauce

To serve 4:

GREEN PEPPER SAUCE:

4	tablespoons butter
3	shallots, chopped
1	large green pepper, seeded and cut into strips
½	cup chicken stock *(pages 194–195)*
2	cups heavy cream
¼	cup mashed potatoes
	Salt and pepper
8	live crayfish (for garnish, *see* **NOTES**)
4	large (about 2 pounds in all) porgy fillets, with the skin left on *(see* **NOTES***)*

NOTES: *Sea bass, rockfish, and snapper are other fish that would work well in this dish. Crayfish are seasonal shellfish, available only from spring to* *autumn, and even when they are in season, they are often difficult to find. Medium-size shrimp can be substituted, or the garnish can be omitted altogether. Ed.*

GREEN PEPPER SAUCE:

Melt the butter in a small frying pan, add the chopped shallots, and cook over low heat for 2 minutes. Add the green pepper strips and sauté over low heat for 10 minutes.

In a small saucepan, boil the chicken stock until it has reduced to about 1 tablespoon of syrupy glaze. Add the cream and stir well to combine. Pour the mixture into an electric blender or a food processor, add the pepper strip mixture, and blend for 2 minutes. Add the mashed potatoes and whir to combine. Return the sauce to the saucepan and season to taste with salt and pepper.

❡ NOTE: *The recipe can be prepared ahead to this point. Ed.*

Preheat the broiler.

Bring a saucepan of water to a boil. Add the crayfish and cook them until they have turned red, about 2 minutes. Drain and keep warm. Reheat the sauce.

Season the fish fillets with salt and pepper, put them on an oiled broiling rack, and broil until just done, about 3 minutes on each side.

Pour some of the sauce onto each plate and the rest into a sauceboat. Put a fillet in the middle of each plate, skin side up, garnish with the crayfish, and serve immediately.

Sabayon de Saint-Pierre en infusion de poivre

Baked John Dory with Pepper Sabayon

To serve 4:

½   shallot, finely chopped
     One 2½-pound John Dory *(see NOTE)*
     Salt and pepper
¾   cup fish stock *(pages 196–197)*

PEPPER SABAYON:

     Cooking liquid from above
1   teaspoon crushed peppercorns
2   egg yolks

NOTE: *Almost any lean fish can be cooked in this way and will be complemented by the sabayon sauce. Ed.*

Preheat the oven to 425° F.

Spread the shallot in a baking dish, put in the fish, sprinkle it with salt and pepper, and add the fish stock. Cover the dish with aluminum foil and bake in the preheated oven basting several times as it cooks, for 20 to 30 minutes, depending on how thick the fish is. Remove the fish to a platter.

PEPPER SABAYON:

Strain the cooking liquid into a heavy-based saucepan, add the crushed peppercorns, and boil to reduce it while you fillet the fish. Skin the fish and lift the fillets off the bones. Moisten the fish with a spoonful or two of the hot cooking liquid and keep warm.

Measure the reduced cooking liquid, pour ½ cup back into the saucepan, and set over very low heat. In a small bowl, whisk together the egg yolks and 3 tablespoons cold water until the mixture expands in volume and is foamy. Off the heat, whisk this sabayon rapidly into the hot cooking liquid and then cook, still whisking, just until the sauce thickens lightly. Remove from the heat.

Transfer the fish fillets to individual plates, pour the sauce over them, and serve immediately.

Papillotes de saumon à l'étuvée de légumes

Salmon Papillotes

To serve 4:

VEGETABLE GARNISH:

1	onion
4	mushrooms
3½	tablespoons butter
1½	carrots, grated
	Salt and pepper
1	teaspoon chopped fresh tarragon *(see page 212 for substitution)*

1¼	pounds salmon fillets
2	tablespoons peanut oil
	Salt and pepper
½	shallot, chopped
2	tablespoons butter
12	fresh tarragon leaves
½	cup white wine
¼	cup chicken stock *(pages 194–195)*

Four 4-inch rounds aluminum foil

VEGETABLE GARNISH:

Cut the onion and the mushrooms into thin slices and then cut the slices into julienne strips. In a saucepan, melt the butter, add the carrots and onion, and sauté over low heat for 5 minutes. Then add the strips of mushroom and cook for 3 more minutes. While the vegetables are cooking, stir them from time to time to prevent them from sticking or browning; they should not color. Sprinkle with salt and pepper, add the tarragon, cover the pan, and simmer over very low heat for 2 minutes. Remove from the heat and set aside.

With tweezers, remove any little bones remaining in the salmon fillets. Cut the fillets into a total of 12 slices, each a little less than ½ inch thick.

Brush the rounds of aluminum foil with the oil. Spoon ¼ of the vegetable garnish onto one half of each foil round. Put the salmon slices on top, sprinkle with salt and pepper and the shallot, dot with butter, and place a tarragon leaf on top of each slice of salmon. Turn up the edges of the foil to catch the liquid and add 2 tablespoons of white wine and 1 tablespoon of stock to each serving.

Fold the loose half of foil over each serving. Then fold and double-fold the edges of foil to make well-sealed, crescent-shaped packages.

❡ NOTE: *The recipe can be prepared ahead to this point. Ed.*

Preheat the oven to 500° F.

Bake the packages in the preheated oven for 2 minutes. Remove them, put on individual plates, and serve. The diners open their own packages so that they can enjoy the concentrated aroma of the first burst of steam.

NOTE: These papillotes are delicious served with lime-flavored white butter sauce (*pages 199–200*).

Bouillabaisse de morue

Salt Cod Stew

To serve 4 to 6:

1½	pounds skinless and boneless salt cod
6	tablespoons olive oil
1	small onion, finely chopped
2	leeks, white part only, well washed and finely chopped
1	garlic clove, finely chopped
1	cup chopped fresh tomatoes *(page 204)*
⅔	pound potatoes
	Pepper
	Pinch saffron (optional)
	Bouquet garni
1	tablespoon tomato paste
½	cup white wine

CROÛTONS:

Twenty ½-inch-thick slices French bread (about 2½ inches in diameter)

½ cup olive oil

2 teaspoons finely chopped parsley

Soak the salt cod in cold water for 12 hours or overnight, changing the water once or twice.

Heat the olive oil in a large heavy flameproof casserole and add the chopped onion, leeks, and garlic. Cook the vegetables over low heat until they are quite soft but not brown, about 15 minutes. Stir in the chopped tomatoes and remove the casserole from the heat.

Peel the potatoes and cut them into ¼-inch slices. Layer the potatoes over the vegetable mixture. Drain the salt cod and pat it dry between paper towels. Cut it into 1½-inch pieces and add them to the casserole. Season with pepper and add the saffron and the bouquet garni. Dissolve the tomato paste in the wine and pour it and 2 cups water over the fish. Simmer the stew on top of the stove over medium heat, uncovered, until the potatoes are tender, about 25 minutes.

CROÛTONS:

Brush both sides of the bread slices with the olive oil and brown them under the broiler on both sides. The surfaces should be crisp, the insides still slightly soft.

When the potatoes are tender, remove the bouquet garni and sprinkle the stew with the chopped parsley. Serve directly from the casserole, accompanied by the croûtons.

Les volailles

POULTRY

Ailerons de volaille au Meursault et aux concombres

Chicken Wings with Cucumbers and White-Wine Sauce

To serve 4:

5½	pounds chicken wings
¾	pound cucumber, peeled, seeded, and cut into 1-inch-long rectangles
5	tablespoons butter
	Salt and pepper
½	shallot, finely chopped
3	ounces mushrooms, finely chopped (about ¾ cup)
¼	cup dry vermouth
⅔	cup Meursault or other white wine
1⅓	cups heavy cream
2	tablespoons chopped fresh tomatoes *(page 204)*
½	teaspoon finely chopped fresh tarragon *(see page 212 for substitution)*
2	teaspoons finely chopped fresh chervil *(see page 212 for substitution)*
1	teaspoon sugar

Only the drumstick-shaped portion of the wing is used in this recipe. Cut these pieces from the wings and save the rest of the wings for stock. With a meat cleaver, cut off the knobby ends of the bones of each chicken-wing "drumstick." It is important to cut off both knobby extremities so that the remainder of the bones can be easily removed later.

Drop the wing pieces into a large pot of unsalted boiling water, boil for 3 minutes, and drain. When the wings are cool enough to handle, remove their bones by pushing one end of each bone with your thumb and pulling it out at the other end of the wing meat.

Cook the cucumber pieces in boiling salted water for 3 minutes and drain.

In a large frying pan, heat 3 tablespoons of the butter and add the boned wings and a little salt and pepper. Cook them slowly for 5 minutes, turn, and cook another 5 minutes. Remove the wings, add the shallot and mushrooms to the pan, and sauté for 3 minutes over medium heat. Add the vermouth and white wine. Scrape the bottom of the pan to dissolve the coagulated pan juices and boil until the liquid is reduced by three fourths. Add the cream, tomatoes, tarragon, 1 teaspoon of the chervil, and salt and pepper. Continue boiling until the sauce is reduced by one half. Lower the heat and add the wings to the sauce.

Melt the remaining 2 tablespoons butter in a frying pan and sauté the cucumber until golden on all sides. Then sprinkle with the sugar and continue browning for 2 minutes more.

Put the wings and the sauce on individual plates or a serving platter. Surround them with the sautéed cucumber, sprinkle with the remaining 1 teaspoon chervil, and serve.

Blancs de volaille au sabayon de poireau

Stuffed Chicken Breasts with Leek Sauce

To serve 4:

VEGETABLE STUFFING:

2½	tablespoons butter
1	carrot, finely chopped
½	onion, finely chopped
2	mushrooms, finely chopped

1 large (¾-ounce) truffle, finely chopped (optional)

Salt and pepper

Pinch thyme flowers or leaves

4 boned chicken breasts

2 teaspoons butter

1 small leek, white part only, well washed and thinly sliced

½ shallot, finely chopped

½ cup tightly packed watercress leaves

2 tablespoons port

1 cup chicken stock *(pages 194–195)*

1 cup *crème fraîche (page 206)*

Salt and pepper

2 egg yolks

VEGETABLE STUFFING:

Heat the 2½ tablespoons butter in a small saucepan. Add the carrot and cook over medium heat for 3 minutes. Then add the onion, stir, and cook for 3 minutes more. Finally add the mushrooms and truffle, if using, and continue cooking, stirring the vegetables frequently during this time to keep them from sticking to the pan, for 3 minutes longer. Season with salt and pepper and thyme.

Remove the skin from the chicken breasts. Make a slit in the side of each breast and cut to form a pocket. Fill the breasts with the vegetable stuffing.

Heat the 2 teaspoons butter in a large frying pan and add the leek and shallot. Cook over medium heat stirring frequently, for 10 minutes. Do not let brown. Add the watercress, port, chicken stock, and *crème fraîche* and boil slowly for another 10 minutes. Reduce the heat, gently put the stuffed chicken breasts in the simmering liquid, and cook slowly, turning them over once, for 10 minutes. Remove the chicken from the pan and keep warm.

Pour all the ingredients remaining in the pan into a food processor or an electric blender. Whir until smooth, pour into a small saucepan, bring almost to a boil, and keep warm over low heat. Adjust the seasoning if necessary.

In a small bowl, beat the egg yolks and 3 tablespoons cold water with a wire whisk until foamy and increased in volume. Pour the yolks into the very hot (but not boiling) sauce, whisking constantly.

Put the stuffed chicken breasts on individual plates, pour the sauce over them, and serve immediately.

NOTES: Only the white of the leek is used since the green leaves would give a bitter taste to the sauce. The beautiful green color of the sauce is due to the watercress, not to the leeks. If you skin the breasts yourself, save the skin and use it in salads. Cut it into little squares, brown in olive oil until crisp, and sprinkle over greens. The only thing that could improve this recipe is one more very large, 1-ounce truffle cut into very fine julienne strips and added with the egg yolks when finishing the sauce.

Ma poule à moi

Michel's Own Chicken

To serve 4:

    One 3-pound chicken, quartered

    Salt and pepper

8   small leeks, white part only, well washed

8   baby carrots

4   baby turnips

4   small onions

    Bouquet garni

1   quart heavy cream

¼   cup vermouth

2   tablespoons fresh chervil leaves *(see page 212 for substitutions)*

Season the chicken pieces well with salt and pepper. Put the chicken legs, the vegetables, and the bouquet garni into a large casserole or Dutch oven. Add the cream and the vermouth and bring to a simmer. Skim off any scum that rises to the surface of the cooking liquid and simmer, uncovered, for 25 minutes. Add the chicken breast sections and cook until all of the chicken pieces are done, about 10 minutes longer.

Transfer the chicken pieces to a serving platter and surround them with the vegetables. Discard the bouquet garni. Season the sauce with salt and pepper, spoon some of it over the chicken, and pour the remaining sauce into a sauceboat. Scatter the fresh chervil leaves over the chicken and serve at once.

NOTE: *The quantity of cream needed to cover the chicken results in an abundance of sauce, but leftover sauce should pose no problem. Combined with chicken stock, it makes an excellent soup, or use the chicken-and-vegetable-flavored cream in virtually any savory recipe that calls for cream. Ed.*

Poulet en cocotte d'argile, sauce hachée

Chicken Cooked in Clay with Herbed Ham and Egg Vinaigrette

To serve 4:

One 3-pound chicken

Salt and pepper

4   medium carrots

4   medium turnips

4   small leeks, trimmed and well washed

Bouquet garni

4   medium potatoes

SAUCE:

2   tablespoons Dijon mustard

2   tablespoons wine vinegar

Salt and pepper

¾   cup olive oil

1   tablespoon each finely chopped fresh chervil, tarragon, and flat-leaf parsley *(see page 212 for substitutions)*

1   hard-cooked egg, finely chopped

⅓   cup finely diced country-cured ham

Römertopf or other unglazed clay pot with a lid

NOTE: The slow cooking allows the flavors to mingle beautifully and smother the chicken, resulting in an extremely flavorful cooking liquid.

Soak the Römertopf or clay pot and lid in water for at least 20 minutes.

Season the chicken with salt and pepper and put it in the pot. Fit the carrots, turnips, and leeks around the chicken and put the bouquet garni and potatoes on top. Cover the pot and put it into a cold oven. Turn the heat to 375° F. and bake the chicken and vegetables for 1 hour and 30 minutes.

SAUCE:

In a bowl, whisk together the mustard, the vinegar, and salt and pepper. Whisk in the oil, a little at a time. When all the oil has been incorporated, the sauce will be quite thick. Stir in the herbs, the chopped egg, and the diced ham. Taste and add more seasoning, if needed. Pour the sauce into a sauceboat.

When the chicken is done, transfer it to a cutting board and cut it into quarters. Arrange the chicken pieces on a serving platter and surround them with the vegetables. Pour the cooking juices from the pot into a second sauceboat. Serve the chicken accompanied by the two sauces.

Le poulet aux endives

Chicken with Endives

To serve 4:

One 3-pound chicken, cut into 8 pieces

Salt and pepper

2   tablespoons butter

3   carrots, chopped

4   shallots, chopped

1   garlic clove, chopped

½   onion, chopped

2½   cups chicken stock *(pages 194–195)*

1   teaspoon tomato paste

Bouquet garni

1½   ounces pimiento

⅔   cup *crème fraîche (page 206)*

GARNISH:

2   endives

1   tablespoon butter

¼   teaspoon sugar

Salt and pepper

Season the chicken pieces with salt and pepper. Heat the 2 tablespoons butter in a large sauté pan. Add the chicken to the pan, skin side down, and sauté until lightly browned, about 5 minutes. Remove the breast and wing pieces from the pan and turn the drumsticks and thighs over to brown the other sides. Add the chopped carrots, shallots, garlic, and onion and sauté for 3 minutes. Add the chicken stock, tomato paste, and bouquet garni, and simmer, uncovered, until the chicken is almost done, about 30 minutes. Return the breast and wing pieces and continue cooking the chicken until all the pieces are tender, about 15 minutes. Remove the chicken pieces from the sauté pan and keep them warm. Discard the bouquet garni.

Pour the contents of the sauté pan into a food processor or an electric blender, add the pimiento and *crème fraîche,* and purée until smooth. Transfer the sauce to a small saucepan and cook over low heat for 5 minutes. Season to taste.

GARNISH:

Cut the endives lengthwise into julienne strips 2 inches long and ⅛-inch wide. In a small frying pan, cook the 1 tablespoon butter until it is brown. Add the endives and the sugar, season with salt and pepper, and sauté for 2 minutes.

Cut the wings in half at the joint. Remove the breast meat from the bones and cut it lengthwise into thin slices. Arrange the chicken drumsticks, thighs, and wing sections in the center of a serving platter and coat with some of the sauce. Pour the remaining sauce into a sauceboat. Arrange the breast slices over the sauced pieces. Surround the chicken with the sautéed endives and serve, accompanied by the remaining sauce.

Volaille "truffée" au persil

Roast Chicken or Game Bird with Parsley

To serve 4:

PARSLEY GARNISH:

5   tablespoons chopped parsley

1   tablespoon chopped chives

2   teaspoons chopped fresh tarragon *(see page 212 for substitution)*

2   shallots, finely chopped

2   mushrooms, finely chopped

1   tablespoon *fromage blanc (page 206)*

   Salt and pepper

2½   pound bird (chicken, guinea hen, or pheasant)

   Salt and pepper

1   teaspoon peanut oil

SAUCE:

¾   cup chicken stock *(pages 194–195)*

1   garlic clove, unpeeled but crushed

1   tablespoon chopped parsley

   Salt and pepper

PARSLEY GARNISH:

Crush all the ingredients for the parsley garnish together in a mortar to form a paste. Or, purée them in a blender or food processor.

Preheat the oven to 425° F.

Working from the neck opening, gently separate the skin from the meat with your fingers. Spread the parsley mixture as evenly as possible between the skin and the meat and pat the skin back into place. Salt and pepper the inside of the bird, truss it, and brush the bird with the oil.

Roast the bird for 20 minutes, turn the heat down to 350° F., and continue roasting until the juices run clear with no trace of pink when tested, about 40 minutes longer. Remove the bird to a carving board and let it stand in a warm place.

SAUCE:

Discard the fat from the roasting pan. On top of the stove over low heat, add to the pan the ¾ cup stock, the garlic, and 1 tablespoon parsley. Stir and scrape all the brown glaze into the sauce. Reduce the sauce by about one third, strain it into a small saucepan, and taste for seasoning.

Quarter the bird, arrange the pieces on a deep platter, pour the sauce over them, and serve.

Poulet au vinaigre de vin

Chicken with Wine-Vinegar Sauce

To serve 4:

One 3-pound chicken, quartered

Salt and pepper

4   tablespoons butter

6   garlic cloves, unpeeled

⅓   cup red–wine vinegar

2½ tablespoons armagnac or cognac

2   teaspoons Dijon mustard

  1   teaspoon tomato paste

  ⅔   cup *crème fraîche (page 206)*

  ¼   cup chopped fresh tomatoes *(page 204)*

  1   teaspoon fresh chervil leaves *(see page 212 for substitution)*

Season the chicken with salt and pepper. Heat 2 tablespoons of the butter in a large frying pan. Put the chicken, skin side down, into the pan and brown for 5 minutes. Turn the pieces and brown on the other side for 5 minutes more. Add the garlic, cover the pan, and cook for 20 minutes over low heat. Remove the breasts and continue to cook the legs 5 minutes longer. Pour off half the fat and liquid that has accumulated in the pan.

Put the breasts back into the pan, raise the heat to medium, and pour in the vinegar. Stir well so that all the juices that have caramelized on the bottom of the pan mix into the sauce as the vinegar boils. Boil the vinegar, half covered, until it has reduced by three fourths. Remove the chicken pieces and keep warm.

In a small bowl, whisk together the armagnac, mustard, and tomato paste, pour the mixture into the frying pan, and boil for 5 minutes. Add the *crème fraîche,* whisking constantly. Remove the pan from the heat and whisk in the remaining 2 tablespoons butter, bit by bit. Taste the sauce for salt and pepper and strain.

Put the chicken on individual plates and pour the sauce over them. Scatter the tomatoes and chervil over the chicken and serve immediately.

Poulet grillé au citron

Grilled Chicken with Lemon

To serve 4:

    One 3-pound chicken

4   thin slices bacon

4   tablespoons butter, melted

    Salt and pepper

1   lemon

¾   cup fresh bread crumbs

SAUCE:

½   pound cold butter

1   tablespoon lemon juice

1   tablespoon chopped fresh chervil *(see page 212 for substitution)*

½   teaspoon chopped fresh tarragon *(see page 212 for substitution)*

    Salt and pepper

Cut along one side of the backbone to split the chicken open. Cut along the other side of the backbone to remove it and also cut off the wing tips. With a sharp knife, remove the wishbone and the ribs. Then press down firmly on the breast to flatten the chicken.

Preheat the broiler.

In a frying pan, cook the slices of bacon until they have rendered most of their fat and are golden brown. Loosen the skin from the flesh of the chicken with your fingers and slip the bacon slices between the skin and the flesh—one piece over each breast and one over each leg section. Turn the chicken over and brush the underside with some of the melted butter. Season with salt and pepper and put the chicken in a baking pan, skin side up. Brush the skin side with a little more of the butter and season it. Broil the chicken until brown, 5–10 minutes.

With a sharp paring knife, remove the entire peel, including the white pith, from the lemon. Cut the lemon crosswise into the thinnest possible slices and remove any seeds. Remove the chicken from the broiler and turn the oven down to 350° F. Cover the chicken with the lemon slices. Sprinkle the bread crumbs over the chicken and drizzle the remaining melted butter over the crumbs to moisten them. Bake the chicken in the preheated oven until the crumbs are lightly browned, about 30 minutes.

While the chicken is cooking, bring 3 tablespoons water to a boil in a heavy-based saucepan. Turn the heat down as low as possible and whisk in the cold butter, a little bit at a time. *(See page 199 for complete instructions on making this type of sauce.)* Add the lemon juice and the chopped fresh herbs and season the sauce with salt and pepper. Pour the sauce into a sauceboat.

Remove the chicken from the oven and cut it into quarters. Arrange the pieces on a serving platter and serve at once, accompanied by the sauce.

Volaille en gelée aux grains de poivre

Preserved Chicken in Gelatine with Peppercorns

To serve 4:

4   chicken legs (drumstick and thigh), about 2 pounds in all

Salt

4   slices bacon

12 white peppercorns

1   tablespoon fresh chervil leaves *(see page 212 for substitution)*

1   teaspoon fresh tarragon leaves *(see page 212 for substitution)*

1   cup dry vermouth
1½   teaspoons gelatine
2   cups chicken stock *(pages 194–195)*

A 1½-quart wide-mouthed preserving jar
Large pot for processing (see **NOTES***)*

Salt each piece of chicken lightly all over, rubbing the salt in with your fingers. Wrap a slice of bacon around each chicken leg. Put the legs in a shallow bowl or baking dish and add the peppercorns, chervil, tarragon, and vermouth. Cover with aluminum foil and refrigerate overnight. Turn the pieces of chicken once while they are marinating.

Moisten the gelatine with 1½ tablespoons water. Heat the chicken stock in a saucepan until it is just lukewarm and stir in the gelatine.

Pack the chicken legs into the preserving jar and pour in all the marinade as well as the chicken stock. Seal the jar and place it in a large pot of boiling water. Boil (process) for 2 hours. Let the jar cool in the water. When cool, remove the jar from the water and refrigerate at least until the jelly has set.

To serve, dip the jar into hot water for a few seconds and turn the chicken out onto a serving platter.

NOTES: This is the perfect thing to take on a picnic. Once the chicken has finished cooking, it has been sterilized and can be kept a long time without spoiling. When preserving any food, certain rules should be kept in mind:

1. The jar and the rubber ring that seals the top should be cleaned in boiling water and left to dry before using.
2. The jar should never be completely filled to the brim. Most jars have a level indicator that shows the maximum they can hold.
3. A very large pot must be used when processing. The pot has to be taller than the jar itself; the sides of the jar should be at least an inch from the sides of the pot. Special preserving kettles are available; they usually have a perforated metal plate that sits on the bottom. If you do not have anything comparable, put a thick cloth on the bottom of

your pot so the jar will be protected from the direct heat.

4. The boiling water should cover the jar by about 1 inch. Add more water as needed and put a weight on top of the jar if it won't stand upright.

Pintadeau grillé au citron vert

Grilled Guinea Hen with Lime

To serve 4:

    One 2-pound guinea hen *(see* **NOTES***)*

2   limes

1   orange

2   onions, thinly sliced

6   tablespoons chicken stock *(pages 194–195)*

    Salt and pepper

¼   cup vinegar

    Artificial sweetener equivalent to 1½ teaspoons sugar

1   teaspoon meat glaze *(see* **NOTES***)*

1   teaspoon *crème fraîche (page 206)*

NOTES: *The recipe can also be used for a chicken. Meat glaze (glace de viande) can be purchased in jars at specialty food shops. To make your own see* **NOTE** *page 77. Ed.*

Cut along one side of the backbone to split the guinea hen open. Cut along the other side of the backbone to remove it and cut off the wing tips. With a sharp knife, remove the wishbone and the ribs. Then press down firmly on the breast to flatten the hen.

    Cut the zest from ½ a lime and from ¼ of the orange in thin strips and set aside. Squeeze 3 tablespoons lime juice and 1½ tablespoons orange juice into a dish large enough to hold the hen. Add the onions and chicken stock. Salt and pepper the hen, put it in the dish, and refrigerate, turning once, overnight.

Cut the lime and orange zest lengthwise into very fine julienne strips. Bring a small saucepan of water to a boil. Add the julienned zest, blanch it for 5 minutes, drain, rinse under cold running water, and set aside.

Remove the hen from the marinade. In a saucepan, simmer the marinade over low heat, covered, until the onions are soft. In another saucepan, dissolve the artificial sweetener in the vinegar and simmer for 5 minutes. In a food processor or an electric blender, combine the cooked marinade, meat glaze, *crème fraîche,* and sweetened vinegar. Purée the sauce, taste for seasoning, and correct if needed.

❦ NOTE: *The recipe can be prepared ahead to this point. Ed.*

Peel the second lime completely so that all of the white pith is cut away and cut out the sections from between the membranes. Set aside.

Preheat the broiler.

Prick the skin of the bird well all over to allow the fat to drain out during cooking. Broil, skin side up, for about 20 minutes. Reheat the sauce.

Quarter the hen. Pour a pool of hot sauce on each of 4 plates. Put a piece of hen in the center of each pool, sprinkle with the zests, and decorate the edges of the plates with the lime sections.

Pintadeau au vin de bordeaux et au lard fumé

Bacon-Cloaked Guinea Hen in Red Wine

To serve 4:

One 2½-pound guinea hen, cut into 8 pieces
(see NOTES*)*

Salt and pepper

8   thin slices smoked bacon

MARINADE:

1   bottle red Bordeaux wine

2   medium carrots, chopped

1   small onion, chopped

     Bouquet garni

1   whole clove

1   garlic clove, unpeeled

1   tablespoon peanut oil

2   tablespoons butter

1   tablespoon flour

1   quart chicken stock *(pages 194–195)*

8   small boiling onions

¼   cup *crème fraîche (page 206)*

2   tablespoons cassis (black currant liqueur)

NOTES: *Chicken can be substituted for the guinea hen. For this recipe, cut up the bird in the French way, which is more or less the same as the American way of cutting up fowl with one important exception: Each wing is cut off so as to include a nice chunk of breast meat. Cut right through the breast so a portion of it comes off with the wing. This reduces the size of the breast pieces, enlarges the wing sections, and makes all eight pieces roughly equal in quantity of meat. Ed.*

Season the guinea hen pieces with pepper and wrap them in the bacon slices. Secure the bacon with wooden toothpicks. Combine all of the marinade ingredients in a deep bowl, add the hen pieces, and refrigerate overnight.

The next day, remove the hen pieces from the marinade and dry them well. Strain the marinade and reserve both the liquid and the vegetables. Heat the peanut oil in a large frying pan. Add the hen pieces and sauté until well browned, about 5 minutes on each side. Remove the pieces from the pan and drain them on paper towels.

Melt the butter in a heavy casserole or Dutch oven. Add the hen pieces and the vegetables strained from the marinade and sauté for 2 minutes. Sprinkle with the flour and cook, stirring well with a wooden spoon to distribute the flour evenly, for 4 minutes. Add the chicken stock, the small onions, and the liquid from the marinade. Bring to a boil, then reduce the heat, and simmer, uncovered, until the hen is tender, about 30 minutes.

With a slotted spoon, remove the hen pieces and the small onions from the casserole. Remove and discard the toothpicks, transfer the hen and the onions to an ovenproof dish, and keep warm. Add the *crème fraîche* to the casserole, whisk well to blend, and bring the sauce to a boil. Add the cassis and let the sauce boil until it has reduced by one half—to about 3½ cups. This will take about 20 minutes. Strain the sauce, skim off excess fat, and season to taste.

Transfer the hen pieces to a serving platter or to individual plates and pour some of the strained sauce over them. Pour the rest into a sauceboat. Garnish the hen with the small onions and serve immediately.

NOTES: The cassis enhances both the flavor of the wine and the color of the sauce. For a slightly different effect, the small onions can be browned separately rather than cooked with the hen.

Perdreaux sur un lit de chou

Partridge on a Bed of Cabbage Leaves

To serve 4:

4   young partridges, livers included *(see* **NOTES***)*

Salt and pepper

Four ½-inch-thick slices French bread (about 2½ inches in diameter)

1   garlic clove

4   thin slices fresh pork belly *(see* **NOTES***)*

One 4½-pound head cabbage

¼   pound salted or fresh pork belly

5   teaspoons butter

¼   cup white wine

NOTES: *If the birds do not have their livers, half as many chicken livers can be used instead. Bacon, put in cold water, brought to a boil, and drained, can be used instead of pork belly. Ed.*

In a small bowl, crush the livers into a purée with the prongs of a fork. Salt and pepper lightly. Rub the slices of bread with the garlic and then spread the bread with the livers. Salt and pepper the birds' insides and put one garnished piece of bread inside each partridge. Truss the birds and tie a slice of pork belly across the breast of each.

Cut the head of cabbage into 4 pieces and then cut out the hard central core. Separate the cabbage leaves and rinse them in cold water. Blanch the leaves by boiling in salted water for 10 minutes. Drain.

Cut the pork belly into strips about ¼ inch wide and 2 inches long and blanch in boiling water for 1 minute. Drain.

Melt the butter in a large enameled casserole or other attractive pot and brown the partridges on all sides over moderate heat for 15 minutes. Remove the pork that was tied around each bird and reserve. Continue browning the birds for 1 minute longer to brown the breasts, remove them from the casserole, and keep warm.

Add ¼ cup water and the white wine to the pan; stir to detach the juices that have stuck to the bottom. Add the cabbage leaves and the pieces of pork that have been tied around the partridges, as well as the pork that was blanched earlier. Stir all these ingredients together, salt and pepper lightly, and then cover the casserole and simmer for 5 minutes.

Remove the trussing strings from the birds. Put the birds in the casserole on top of the cabbage, cover, and serve immediately. Or, the birds can be quartered in the kitchen and arranged on individual plates.

NOTE: Squab can be used instead of partridge; it is excellent prepared in this way.

Pot au feu de volaille et de langue de veau
au beurre blanc

Chicken and Veal Tongue with Vegetables and Butter Sauce

To serve 8:

1	fresh veal tongue, soaked in cold water for 30 minutes
	Salt and pepper
2½ to 3	quarts chicken stock *(pages 194–195)*
1	onion, chopped
1	carrot, quartered
	Bouquet garni
	One 3-pound chicken

VEGETABLE GARNISH:

1	small cucumber
16	baby turnips, peeled
16	baby carrots
8	small leeks, well washed
16	asparagus tips
1½	cups white butter sauce *(page 199)*

Bring a saucepan of water to a boil, add the soaked tongue, and cook it for 45 minutes. Remove the tongue from the saucepan and let it cool slightly. Peel the tongue and trim off any fat or gristle from the base.

Preheat the oven to 350° F.

Season the tongue with salt and pepper and put it into a large casserole or Dutch oven. Add chicken stock to cover, the chopped onion, quartered carrot, and bouquet garni and cover the casserole.

Bring to a boil on top of the stove and then cook in the preheated oven for 1 hour and 15 minutes. Add the chicken and more stock if needed and cook for another 45 minutes.

VEGETABLE GARNISH:

Meanwhile, peel the cucumber lengthwise with a citrus stripper, removing about half the peeling so the cucumber looks striped. Bring a large saucepan of salted water to a boil. Add the turnips, carrots, and leeks and boil for 7 minutes. Then add the asparagus tips and cucumber pieces and cook all the vegetables together for 2 minutes longer. Drain the vegetables, refresh them under cold running water, and return to the saucepan.

Just before the chicken and tongue are done, prepare the butter sauce and reheat the vegetables.

Slice the tongue and transfer it to a deep oval serving platter. Cut the chicken into 8 pieces.

(**NOTE:** *When you cut off the wing pieces, include some of the breast so that the chicken yields 8 roughly equal pieces. Ed.)* Ladle a spoonful of the cooking liquid over the meats. Arrange the vegetables around the meats, alternating colors, and serve accompanied by the butter sauce in a sauceboat.

NOTES: *The obvious bonus from this recipe is doubly flavorful stock. Serve as soup or save it to use in another recipe. The combination of chicken, vegetables, and sauce is excellent even without the tongue. Either use 2 chickens to serve 8 or, to serve 4, omit the tongue and halve the quantities of vegetables and sauce. Ed.*

Les viandes & abats

MEATS &
VARIETY MEATS

Rable de lapin aux poivrons rouges

Braised and Steamed Rabbit with Pimiento

To serve 4:

1   tablespoon olive oil

5   medium carrots, chopped

2   shallots, chopped

½   onion, chopped

1   garlic clove, chopped

      One 3-pound rabbit, cut up *(see **NOTE**)*

      Salt and pepper

5   cups chicken stock *(pages 194–195)*

1   teaspoon tomato paste

      Bouquet garni

3   tablespoons diced pimiento

NOTE: *To cut up the rabbit, begin by turning it on its back so you can see where the fleshy portions are. You want to keep the long strips of tender meat on the center section (the saddle) in one piece. Cut off the back legs and split them so you have 2 pieces. Cut off the front section including the legs and most of the ribs but taking care not to cut into the rack meat. Split the front section in two also. Cut away the flaps from the saddle and discard. The 4 leg pieces should be neat, but don't worry if the saddle is less than perfectly attractive since its meat will be removed from the bones before serving. Ed.*

Heat the olive oil in a large frying pan set over low heat. Add the chopped carrots, shallots, onion, and garlic and cook them until soft but not brown, about 8 minutes.

    Season the rabbit legs with salt and pepper and arrange them on top of the softened vegetables in the frying pan. Add the chicken stock, the tomato paste, and the bouquet garni. Bring to a boil, lower the heat, and let bubble gently, uncovered, for 30 minutes. Transfer the cooked rabbit legs to a baking dish, cover with aluminum foil, and keep warm in a preheated 200° F. oven.

Bring the liquid in the pan back to a boil and reduce to about 3 cups. Discard the bouquet garni. Pour the contents of the pan into a food processor or an electric blender and whir until smooth. Pour this sauce into a small pan and keep warm over low heat.

Steam the saddle over boiling water until just cooked, 7 to 8 minutes. (**NOTE:** *Any implement you have or can rig up to steam the rabbit is fine. A fish poacher is good, or a couscous maker, an Oriental steamer, or even a large strainer set in a pot. Just be sure that only steam, not boiling water, touches the meat. Ed.)* Remove the saddle from the steamer, bone it, and cut the meat first in half crosswise and then lengthwise into thin slices.

Put the pieces of braised rabbit on individual plates. Spoon some of the sauce over the legs and pour the rest into a sauceboat. Arrange the rabbit slices, overlapping, across the leg meat and down the bone. Season them with salt and pepper. Garnish with the diced pimiento and serve immediately with the extra sauce.

Côtes de veau en papillote

Veal Chops in Foil

To serve 4:

4   thick veal chops (about 2 pounds in all)
    Salt and pepper
2   tablespoons butter

SAUCE:

1   shallot, finely chopped
2   tablespoons white wine
3   tablespoons port

1   cup *crème fraîche (page 206)*

1½ tablespoons chopped fresh tarragon *(see page 212 for substitution)*

      Salt and pepper

GARNISH:

2   tablespoons butter

2   ounces raw ham, finely diced (about ½ cup)

1   carrot, finely diced

1   medium onion, finely diced

2   ounces mushrooms, finely diced (about ½ cup)

1   small celery rib, finely diced

2   teaspoons dried thyme

      Salt and pepper

1   tablespoon port

1   generous tablespoon *crème fraîche (page 206)* or heavy cream

4   thin slices cooked ham, cut the same size as the chops

4   teaspoons port

Four 12-inch rounds aluminum foil

Season the veal chops with salt and pepper. Melt the butter in a large frying pan set over medium-high heat. When the butter is hot, add the chops and sauté them until lightly browned, about 2 minutes on each side.

SAUCE:

Set the sautéed chops aside, add the chopped shallot to the pan, and sauté until softened. Add the white wine and the 3 tablespoons port, bring to a boil, and stir with a wooden spoon to dislodge any coagulated juices adhering to the bottom of the pan. Stir in the 1 cup *crème fraîche* and the tarragon and simmer until the sauce thickens slightly, about 4 minutes. Season the sauce with salt and pepper and remove the pan from the heat.

GARNISH:

Melt the butter in a medium-size saucepan over medium heat. When the butter is hot, add the diced ham and vegetables and stir in the dried thyme. Season with salt and pepper, cover the saucepan, and cook the mixture for 10 minutes. Remove the lid, stir in the 1 table-spoon port and the *crème fraîche* or heavy cream, cook the mixture for 2 minutes, and set aside.

Preheat the oven to 475° F.

Butter the rounds of foil and spread them out on a work surface. Spoon some of the ham and vegetable garnish onto one half of each foil circle. Put a veal chop on top of the mixture and cover each chop with a slice of ham. Spoon the remaining garnish mixture over the ham and sprinkle 1 teaspoon of port over each chop. Fold the loose half of foil over each chop. Then fold and double fold the edges of foil to make well-sealed, crescent-shaped packages.

❡ **NOTE:** *The recipe can be prepared ahead to this point. Ed.*

Bake the veal chops in the preheated oven for 8 minutes—the pack-ages should inflate. Meanwhile, reheat the sauce. Remove the packages from the oven and put them on individual plates, pour the sauce into a sauceboat, and serve immediately. The diners open their own packages so that they can enjoy the concentrated aroma of the first burst of steam.

Blanquette de veau à la crème d'herbes fines

Veal Fricassee with Fresh Herb Sauce

To serve 4 to 6:

3	pounds boneless veal shoulder, trimmed of fat and gristle and cubed
1½	quarts chicken stock *(pages 194–195)*
4	leeks, white part only, well washed and sliced
2	small carrots, sliced
1	small celery rib, sliced
2	ounces mushrooms, sliced (about ½ cup)
1	medium onion, stuck with 1 whole clove
	Bouquet garni
25	small boiling onions
25	fresh button mushrooms
3	tablespoons butter
⅓	cup flour
3	tablespoons *crème fraîche (page 206)*

TO FINISH:

2	tablespoons *crème fraîche*
2	egg yolks
	Salt and pepper
2	tablespoons chopped mixed fresh herbs: parsley, tarragon, chervil, and basil *(see pages 211–212 for substitutions)*
2	tablespoons fresh chervil leaves *(see page 212 for substitution)*

Put the cubed veal and the chicken stock into a large pot and slowly bring to a boil. With a slotted spoon or skimmer, carefully remove the scum that rises to the surface until no more scum appears. Then add the sliced vegetables, the studded onion, and the bouquet garni and simmer, partially covered, for 1 hour and 30 minutes.

While the meat is cooking, bring a medium saucepan of salted water to a boil. Add the small onions and boil them for 10 minutes. Then add the mushrooms and cook them with the onions for another 5 minutes. Drain the vegetables, return to the saucepan, and set aside.

Melt the butter in a large saucepan set over medium heat. Whisk in the flour and cook the mixture for 3 minutes, whisking constantly. Remove the saucepan from the heat.

When the meat is done, transfer it to a serving platter and keep it warm. Reheat the onions and mushrooms. Strain the stock—there should be 1 quart—and whisk it into the flour and butter *roux*. (**NOTE:** *If the meat has been cooked at a simmer and partially covered, just the right amount of liquid should remain. If there is too little, augment it with water; if too much, cook down to reduce. Ed.*) Set the saucepan over high heat and cook, whisking constantly, for 3 minutes. Whisk in the 3 tablespoons *crème fraîche*. Remove the saucepan from the heat.

❦ **NOTE:** *The recipe can be prepared ahead to this point. Ed.*

Reheat the vegetables, meat, and sauce, if necessary.

TO FINISH:

Beat the 2 tablespoons *crème fraîche* with the egg yolks and whisk this mixture into the sauce. Season the sauce with salt and pepper. Stir in the cooked onions and mushrooms and the chopped fresh herbs. Spoon the vegetables and some of the sauce over the meat and scatter the fresh chervil leaves over the top. Pour the remaining sauce into a sauceboat and serve.

NOTE: A delicious accompaniment is steamed potatoes or buttered noodles.

Escalopes de veau aux crabes

Veal Scallops with Crab and Broccoli

To serve 4:

24 broccoli flowerets

Hollandaise sauce *(page 200)*

Four ⅓-pound veal scallops, pounded to ¼ inch thick

Salt and pepper

½ cup flour

6 tablespoons butter

4 garlic cloves, unpeeled

½ pound (about 1¾ cups) cooked lump crab meat

Bring a pan of salted water to a boil. Add the broccoli flowerets and cook them until just tender, about 3 minutes. Refresh them under cold running water and drain.

Prepare the hollandaise sauce and keep it warm.

Salt and pepper the veal scallops. Dredge them in the flour and shake them to remove any excess. Melt the butter in a large frying pan over medium-high heat and add the garlic cloves. When the butter is hot, add 2 of the veal scallops and sauté them until nicely browned, about 3 minutes on each side. Transfer them to a serving platter and keep them warm. Repeat with the remaining scallops.

Gently heat the crab meat and reheat the broccoli. Pile the crab meat in the center of the scallops and surround the scallops with the broccoli flowerets. Pour the hollandaise sauce over the veal and serve at once.

Côte de boeuf sur le sel au beurre vigneron

Salt-Roasted Rib Steak with Herb Butter

To serve 4:

HERB BUTTER:

1	small shallot, finely chopped
¼	garlic clove, finely chopped
1½	tablespoons white wine
4	tablespoons butter, softened
2	teaspoons finely chopped parsley
2	teaspoons finely chopped fresh chervil *(see page 212 for substitution)*
½	teaspoon lemon juice
	Salt and pepper
	Nutmeg

	One 2½- to 3-pound rib steak *(see* **NOTE***)*
1	tablespoon olive oil
1½	pounds coarse salt
	Salt and pepper

NOTE: The rib steak should be cut from the end of the rib roast closest to the sirloin. Have the butcher cut the large curved bone off the meat but leave the shorter, straight bone attached.

HERB BUTTER:

In a small saucepan, boil the shallot, garlic, and white wine slowly over low heat until the shallot has softened and only about 1 teaspoon of liquid remains, about 2 minutes. Pour the contents of the pan into a bowl and let cool. Add the butter, herbs, lemon juice, salt and pepper, and a grating of nutmeg to the bowl, mix well, and set aside.

Preheat the oven to 450° F.

Flatten the rib steak by slapping it with the side of a cleaver and brush both sides with the oil. Spread the coarse salt over the bottom of a roasting pan, sprinkle with a little water, and put the pan in the oven. Heat until the salt has hardened into a block and has begun to make a quiet crackling sound; this will take at least 30 minutes.

Place the meat on the hot salt and cook for 12 minutes on a side. Halfway through the cooking time of each side, salt and pepper the meat lightly. Let the cooked meat rest in a warm place for 15 minutes.

Put the steak on a cutting board and carve it into 8 slices, holding the knife at about a 30-degree angle to the meat. Salt and pepper the slices and arrange them on a platter, insofar as possible reconstituting the shape of the steak. Spoon the herb butter over the meat and serve.

NOTES: I think the best rib steaks for cooking this way come from a young female animal, slightly fat, that has had no more than one calf.

It is impossible for salt and pepper to ever reach the center of a large piece of meat such as a rib steak, leg of lamb, or even a large fish. That is why I only season meat lightly during cooking and why it is always preferable to salt and pepper it after it has been cut and is ready to serve.

Grillade de boeuf au gros sel

Tournedos Grilled on Coarse Salt

To serve 4:

Coarse salt

4   tournedos, about 1 pound in all *(see* **NOTE***)*

NOTE: *Tournedos are cut from the section of the fillet that is near but not at the very end of the rib end of the whole fillet. Ed.*

Preheat the oven to 500° F.

Completely cover the bottom of a cast-iron skillet with a thin layer of coarse salt. Heat the skillet in the preheated oven until the salt crackles. Remove from the oven and put over high heat. Put the tournedos in the skillet—they will not stick—and cook for 4 minutes on each side.

Grillade de boeuf "aux appétits"

Grilled Tournedos with Shallot and Garlic

To serve 4:

SHALLOT AND GARLIC GARNISH:

1   shallot, finely chopped

1   small clove garlic, finely chopped

2   tablespoons chopped parsley

     Juice of ½ lemon

2   teaspoons olive oil

     Salt and pepper

     Nutmeg

4   tournedos, about 1 pound in all *(see* **NOTE** *in preceding recipe)*

1   teaspoon olive oil

Combine the garnish ingredients and set aside.

Brush the tournedos lightly with the 1 teaspoon olive oil. Heat a cast-iron skillet to very hot and cook the tournedos rapidly for 4 minutes on each side. Put 1 tournedo on each plate, spoon the garnish over each, and serve.

Grillade de boeuf au poivre vert

Grilled Tournedos with Green Peppercorns

To serve 4:

GREEN PEPPERCORN SAUCE:

½   cup white wine

2½ tablespoons armagnac or cognac

4   teaspoons green peppercorns and 2½
    tablespoons of their liquid

¼   cup chicken stock *(pages 194–195)*

1⅓ cups *crème fraîche (page 206)*

    Salt and pepper

½   teaspoon sugar

1   tablespoon red-wine vinegar

4   teaspoons port

1½ tablespoons chopped pimiento

3   tablespoons butter

4   tournedos, about 1 pound in all *(see **NOTE**
    on page 120)*

GREEN PEPPERCORN SAUCE:

In a small saucepan, bring the white wine and armagnac to a boil. Boil slowly, uncovered, until the liquid has reduced by two thirds, about 6 minutes. Add the liquid from the green peppercorns and the stock and continue boiling slowly for 5 minutes. Then add the *crème fraîche* and salt and pepper and boil gently, stirring occasionally, until the liquid has reduced by one third, about 15 minutes.

While the sauce is reducing, boil the sugar and vinegar until the mixture is a dark caramel color and the consistency of a light syrup, about 30 seconds. Pour the vinegar-sugar mixture into the sauce once it has been reduced, stir in the port, green peppercorns, and pimiento, and keep warm. Taste for seasoning.

In a heavy frying pan, melt the butter over medium-high heat and sauté the tournedos until medium rare, about 4 minutes per side. Put a tournedo on each plate, top with the sauce, and serve.

Grillade de boeuf au poivre vert minceur

Minceur Grilled Tournedos with Green Peppercorns

To serve 4:

GREEN PEPPERCORN SAUCE:

½ cup white wine

2 tablespoons armagnac or cognac

½ cup chicken stock *(pages 194–195)*

4 teaspoons green peppercorns and a little of their juice

2 mushrooms

1 cup milk made with nonfat dry milk and water

4 teaspoons *fromage blanc (page 206)*

2 tablespoons chopped pimiento

4 tournedos, about 1 pound in all *(see* **NOTE** *on page 120)*

Coarse salt or 1 teaspoon olive oil

GREEN PEPPERCORN SAUCE:

In a small saucepan, simmer the white wine and armagnac until reduced to a couple of tablespoons. Then add a few drops of the juice from the can of green peppercorns and the stock. Simmer over low heat for 10 minutes.

In another saucepan, cook the mushrooms in the milk over low heat for 10 minutes. In a food processor or an electric blender, purée the mushrooms with half their cooking liquid and the *fromage blanc*. Stir this liaison into the reduced stock and add the green peppercorns and the pimiento. Taste for seasoning and keep the sauce warm.

Either cook the beef as for tournedos grilled on coarse salt (*page 120*) or brush the steaks lightly with the oil and cook rapidly in a cast-iron skillet for 4 minutes on each side.

Pièce de boeuf sautée au bordeaux

Steak with Red-Wine Sauce

To serve 2:

5½	tablespoons butter
	One 1¼-pound sirloin steak
1	small shallot, finely chopped
¼	cup red wine, preferably Bordeaux
½	cup chicken stock (*pages 194–195*)

In a heavy frying pan, melt 1½ tablespoons of the butter over medium-high heat and sauté the steak until medium rare, about 4 minutes on each side. Remove from the pan.

Make the sauce: Reduce the heat to medium and stir in the shallot. Add the wine, stir to dislodge the coagulated juice in the pan, and boil until three-fourths of the wine has evaporated. Add the stock and continue boiling to reduce the liquid by half. Off the heat add the remaining 4 tablespoons butter, bit by bit, shaking the pan to incorporate each piece. Pour the sauce over the steak, straining it or not as you like, and serve.

Grillade de palette de boeuf à la marinade

Grilled Beef with Seasoned Butter

To serve 4:

1¾   pounds blade steak, or boneless chuck *(see* **NOTES***)*

3   tablespoons olive oil

4   tablespoons peanut oil

3   tablespoons red wine

SEASONED BUTTER:

6   ounces butter, softened

1   shallot, chopped

5   tablespoons white wine

1   teaspoon finely chopped fresh tarragon *(see page 212 for substitution)*

3   anchovy fillets

    Pinch finely chopped garlic

    Salt and pepper

2   teaspoons Dijon mustard

2   teaspoons lemon juice

2   teaspoons armagnac or cognac

2   teaspoons Worcestershire sauce

    Salt and pepper

1   tablespoon finely chopped parsley

NOTES: The cut of meat used in this recipe is sometimes called *le morceau du boucher* (the butcher's cut) in France because only a few people realize how good it is. Not as tender as a sirloin steak, this cut

has more flavor and marinating makes it quite tender indeed. The
blade, or boneless chuck, is just above the shoulder blade and at the
base of the neck. In France, this cut usually has a piece of gristle running down the middle. This band of gristle is removed, which makes
two long, thin pieces of meat each about 14 inches long, 5 inches
wide, and 2 inches thick. In order to have 1¾ pounds of gristle-free
meat, you may have to buy 2¼ pounds of chuck or blade. These
steaks can be broiled whole as described in this recipe or cut into individual steaks before cooking. Other cuts of meat can be marinated and
cooked this way—bottom round, for instance.

Put the meat on a large, deep platter with the olive oil, 3 tablespoons
of the peanut oil, and the red wine. Cover the platter with aluminum
foil and refrigerate for at least 24 hours before cooking. Turn the meat
over once every 12 hours.

SEASONED BUTTER:
Melt 2 teaspoons of the butter in a small saucepan and add the shallot,
white wine, and tarragon. Boil slowly, stirring constantly, for 3 minutes, until the shallot has softened and there are only about 2 tablespoons of the mixture left in the pan. Remove the pan from the heat
and let cool. Spoon the shallot mixture into a food processor or an
electric blender and add the anchovies, garlic, salt and pepper, mustard, lemon juice, armagnac, and Worcestershire sauce. Process or
blend until smooth, add the remaining butter, and whir until combined. Set aside at room temperature.

Preheat the broiler.
Take the meat from the marinade, dry it with paper towels, and
then brush it with the remaining 1 tablespoon peanut oil. Put the meat
in the hot broiler and cook until it is springy to the touch, 4 to 5
minutes a side.
Once the meat is cooked, cut it into 4 pieces. Salt and pepper the
pieces, put each one on a plate, and spread with a spoonful of the
seasoned butter. Sprinkle with the chopped parsley and serve immediately. Serve the remaining butter in a separate small bowl.

Carré d'agneau persillé

Parslied Rack of Lamb

To serve 4:

2   racks of lamb, chined *(see NOTE)*
3   garlic cloves, unpeeled
    Salt and pepper

COATING:

2   tablespoons chopped parsley
2   garlic cloves, finely chopped
½   cup fresh bread crumbs
2   tablespoons Dijon mustard

¾   cup chicken stock *(pages 194–195)* or cold water

NOTE: *The racks are the two rib sections. Ask the butcher to remove the shoulder blade bone and to saw through and remove the chunky part of the backbone, the chine, that is attached to the racks. This will facilitate carving. Have the bones chopped and reserve them to enrich the cooking juices. Ed.*

If necessary, remove the parchment-like fell covering the fatty sides of the racks and trim the fat to a layer ⅓ inch thick.

Preheat the oven to 475° F.

Put the chopped bones into a large roasting pan and add the unpeeled garlic cloves. Season the racks with salt and pepper and set them, fat side up, on top of the chopped bones. Roast them in the preheated oven for 20 minutes, basting them once or twice with the fat that accumulates in the pan.

COATING:

Meanwhile, combine the chopped parsley and garlic with the fresh bread crumbs. Remove the lamb from the oven and spread the mustard over the fatty sides of the racks. Sprinkle the coated surfaces with the parsley mixture and return the racks to the oven until a nice brown crust forms, about 10 minutes. Put the racks on a serving platter and let rest in a warm place while you make the sauce.

Drain off any excess fat in the roasting pan. Deglaze the pan by pouring in the chicken stock or water and whisking well to dislodge any coagulated juices adhering to the bottom. Continue cooking until the liquid has reduced by one half and then strain the sauce into a sauceboat.

Carve the racks at the table, slicing down between the bones to cut into neat chops.

Comment réussir votre gigot d'agneau rôti

Roast Leg of Lamb

To serve 4:

> One 4-pound leg of lamb (shank half)
> 2 tablespoons peanut oil
> 2 tablespoons butter, softened
> 6 garlic cloves, unpeeled
> 1 cup chicken stock (*pages 194–195*)
> 6 tablespoons cold butter (optional)

If necessary, remove the parchment-like fell covering the leg and trim the fat to a layer ⅓ inch thick.

Preheat the oven to 475° F.

Rub the lamb with the oil and the softened butter, put it in a roasting pan, and surround it with the garlic cloves. Roast the lamb in the preheated oven, basting the leg and turning it over every 10 minutes. When the lamb is medium rare (140° F.) on a meat thermometer, after about 50 minutes, transfer it to a carving board and cover it loosely with aluminum foil. Let the meat rest in a warm place for 20 to 30 minutes.

Meanwhile, pour any excess fat out of the roasting pan, add the chicken stock, and bring to a boil. Stir well to dislodge and dissolve any juices that have coagulated on the bottom and continue cooking until the sauce has reduced by one half. Strain it, pressing hard on the garlic cloves with the back of a spoon to extract all their juices. For a richer sauce, whisk in the cold butter, a little bit at a time so it softens, thickening the sauce lightly. Pour into a sauceboat, carve the lamb, and serve.

NOTE: Letting the lamb rest before carving allows the meat to relax. The blood, which has retreated to the center, flows back to the extremities, resulting in a roast that is tender and uniformly rosy pink.

Jambon au coulis de champignons

Ham with Mushroom and Sorrel Sauce

To serve 4:

1   pound boneless ham, cut into ¼-inch slices
     Pepper
¼   cup white wine
½   cup fresh or frozen tiny green peas

MUSHROOM AND SORREL SAUCE:

1   tablespoon butter
½   pound mushrooms, quartered
1   large shallot, chopped
⅓   cup white wine

6   tablespoons white port

1   cup *crème fraîche* (*page 206*)

2   ounces fresh sorrel leaves, cut into very thin
strips (about 2 cups)

Preheat the oven to 325° F.

Butter the bottom of an attractive baking dish large enough to hold the ham in a single layer. Add the slices of ham, season them with pepper, and pour the ¼ cup white wine over them. Cover the dish tightly with aluminum foil and put the ham into the preheated oven to warm gently.

Bring a small saucepan of salted water to a boil and add the peas. Cook them for 15 minutes if using fresh peas, 6 minutes if frozen. Remove the peas with a slotted spoon and transfer them to a strainer set over the cooking liquid to keep them warm.

MUSHROOM AND SORREL SAUCE:

Melt the 1 tablespoon butter in a medium-size saucepan, add the mushrooms and the chopped shallot, and cook them for 2 minutes without letting them brown. Pour the ⅓ cup wine into the saucepan and bring to a boil. When the liquid in the pan has almost evaporated, after about 6 minutes, add the port and the *crème fraîche* and boil for 4 minutes. Pour this mixture into an electric blender or a food processor and purée until smooth and frothy, about 2 minutes. Pour the sauce back into the saucepan, stir in the sorrel, and boil the sauce for 30 seconds.

Remove the ham from the oven and drain off and discard the cooking liquid. Pour the sauce over the ham and scatter the cooked peas over the top. Serve directly from the baking dish.

Langue de boeuf à la fondue d'oignons

Baby Beef Tongue Braised with Onions

To serve 4 or 5:

One 1½- to 2-pound calf's tongue

1½ cups red wine

Salt and pepper

¾ pound onions, thinly sliced

2 tomatoes, cut in half and seeded

Bouquet garni, including 1 garlic clove, unpeeled but crushed

1 tablespoon each finely chopped fresh tarragon and chervil (*see page 212 for substitutions*)

1 cup chicken stock (*pages 194–195*)

NOTE: *Either baby beef or calf's tongue can be used in this recipe. Ed.*

In a large saucepan, first parboil the tongue in unsalted boiling water for 10 or 15 minutes. In a small saucepan, simmer the wine until it is reduced by one half.

Preheat the oven to 400° F.

Sprinkle the tongue with salt and pepper and put it in a casserole just large enough to hold it. Cover the tongue with the sliced onions and add the tomatoes, bouquet garni, half the chopped herbs, the reduced red wine, and the chicken stock. Braise the tongue, covered, in the preheated oven until very tender, about 2 hours.

Lift the tongue from the casserole and skin it, removing also any pieces of gristle and bone at the root. Keep it warm. Discard the bouquet garni and purée the braising liquid and vegetables in a food processor or an electric blender. Reheat the sauce and taste for seasoning.

Cut the tongue into thin slices and arrange them close together on a platter to approximate the original shape. Pour the sauce around the tongue and sprinkle the remaining tarragon and chervil over all.

Pot au feu de langues

Boiled Tongues with Vegetables and Tomato Sauce

To serve 4 to 6:

One 2¼-pound beef tongue, roots removed

One 1¼-pound calf's tongue, roots removed

Salt and pepper

3   quarts chicken stock (*pages 194–195*)

1   onion, sliced

1   carrot, sliced

Bouquet garni

12   baby carrots

12   baby turnips, peeled

6   small leeks, white part only

6   very small potatoes

Six 1½-inch-thick slices cucumber, seeds scooped out

16   asparagus tips

ACCOMPANIMENTS:

Fresh tomato sauce (*page 201*)

Small bowl of coarse salt

Dijon mustard

Sour gherkins (*cornichons*)

Pickled onions

Soak the tongues in a large bowl of cold water for 3 hours before cooking them. Change the water every hour or place the bowl in the sink and let a small stream of cold water run into the bowl for the full 3 hours.

Drain the tongues, put them in a large pot, and add enough cold water to cover. Do not salt. Bring the water to a boil and then boil slowly, uncovered, for 30 minutes. Skim whatever foam rises to the surface while the tongues are boiling.

Preheat the oven to 400° F.

Drain the tongues, discarding the water, cool them, and peel off the rough skin that covers them. Salt and pepper the tongues, put them back in the pot, and add the stock, onion, carrot, and bouquet garni. Cover the pot and cook in the preheated oven for 2 hours.

Thirty minutes before the tongues have finished cooking, tie the carrots, turnips, and leeks in a piece of cheesecloth and add them to the pot. Ten minutes later, start boiling the potatoes in a saucepan of salted water. Wrap the cucumber and asparagus in another piece of cheesecloth and add them to the pot with the tongue 10 minutes before the 2-hour cooking time is up.

To serve, lift the tongues out of their cooking liquid and cut each one into ¼-inch slices. Arrange them close together on a platter to approximate the original shapes of the tongues. Unwrap the 2 packets of vegetables and arrange them around the edge of the platter, alternating colors. Place a small potato inside each of the hollowed-out slices of cucumber. Spoon a little of the cooking liquid over the meat and serve, accompanied by the fresh tomato sauce, a bowl of coarse salt, Dijon mustard, *cornichons,* and pickled onions.

NOTES: The liquid the tongues cooked in should not be discarded. Skim the fat off the surface and serve the delicious bouillon as a soup before serving the tongue. The bouillon can be served as it is or in one of the following ways:

1. with croûtons and grated cheese,
2. with 2 tablespoons of Bordeaux wine added to each bowl just before serving,
3. with a teaspoon of *crème fraîche* and a teaspoon of port added to each serving along with an egg, which will poach slowly in the soup, which must be very hot.

Piccatas de foie de veau en vinaigrette de têtes d'asperges

Sautéed Veal Liver with Asparagus Vinaigrette

To serve 4:

24 thin young asparagus spears

½ cup vinaigrette gourmande (*page 203*)

3 tablespoons red-wine vinegar

⅓ cup chicken stock (*page 194–195*)

Salt and pepper

4 slices veal liver (about 1 pound in all)

2 tablespoons fresh chervil leaves (*see page 212 for substitution*)

Bring a large saucepan of salted water to a boil. Snap off the tough stem ends from the asparagus and peel the stalks. Cut off the stalks 1½ inches below the tips and reserve the stalks. With a sharp paring knife, trim the cut end of the tips to give them a rounded shape. Cook the stalks in the boiling water for 9 minutes. Lift them out of the water with a slotted spoon, refresh them under cold running water, and drain them well. In the same water, boil the asparagus tips for 3 minutes. Refresh them under cold running water, drain well, and set aside.

Purée the stems in a food processor or an electric blender and then strain the purée. Return the asparagus purée to the processor or blender, add the vinaigrette, vinegar, and chicken stock, and whir to combine. Season the sauce with salt and pepper.

❮ NOTE: *The recipe can be prepared ahead to this point. Ed.*

Transfer the sauce to a saucepan and set over very low heat. Reheat the asparagus tips. Heat a nonstick frying pan, add the liver slices, and sauté them until browned but still pink within, just 1 to 2 minutes on each side. *(NOTE: If you don't have a nonstick pan, use a regular frying pan with 1 to 2 tablespoons of oil. In fact, the liver will brown even better this way. Ed.)* Season the liver with salt and pepper. Pour the asparagus vinaigrette onto four plates. Arrange the sautéed liver and the asparagus tips on the sauce and garnish with the chervil leaves.

Rognon de veau "en habit vert"

Veal Kidney Braised in Spinach and Lettuce Leaves

To serve 4:

2	young veal kidneys (about 1 pound in all)
12	spinach leaves
12	lettuce leaves
	Salt and pepper
2	teaspoons olive oil
1	carrot, sliced
1	leek, white part only, well washed and sliced
1	onion, sliced
1½	cups chicken stock (*pages 194–195*)
	Bouquet garni
2	mushrooms
1½	teaspoons nonfat dry milk
	Nutmeg
1	teaspoon *fromage blanc* (*page 206*)
1	teaspoon Dijon mustard

Remove all the fat and the filament that encase the veal kidneys if the butcher has not already done so and cut out the kernel of fat at the root of each.

Remove the stems of the spinach, blanch the spinach and the lettuce leaves in boiling water for 1 minute, and spread them out flat on a dry cloth to drain. Sprinkle the kidneys with salt and pepper and wrap them in the spinach and lettuce.

Heat the olive oil in a pan large enough to hold the kidneys and in it cook the carrot, leek, and onion until they soften and give off some of their liquid. Add the wrapped kidneys, chicken stock, and bouquet garni and braise the kidneys, covered, over low heat, basting often with the juices in the pan, for 25 to 30 minutes. Do not overcook; when they are done, they should still be pink in the center.

Meanwhile, cut the mushrooms in half and put them in a small saucepan with 2 tablespoons water, the dry milk, salt and pepper, and a grating of nutmeg. Cook over low heat, uncovered, for 15 minutes.

Remove the kidneys and strain the braising liquid into a food processor or an electric blender. Add the cooked mushrooms, *fromage blanc,* and mustard and whir until smooth. Pour this sauce into a small saucepan and reheat it but do not allow it to boil. Adjust seasoning as necessary.

Unwrap the veal kidneys and cut them into very thin slices. Pour a ribbon of sauce around the edges of individual plates, arrange the spinach and lettuce leaves in the center of each, and overlap the slices of kidney on top of them.

Rognons de veau au persil et à la graine de moutarde

Veal Kidneys and Parsley with Mustard Sauce

To serve 4:

PARSLEY GARNISH:

⅔ pound Italian flat-leaf parsley, large stems removed (*see* **NOTE**)

¼ pound spinach leaves, stems removed

2 tablespoons butter

MUSTARD SAUCE:

3 tablespoons butter

2 shallots, finely chopped

6 tablespoons cognac

1 cup chicken stock (*pages 194–195*)

6½ tablespoons *crème fraîche* (*page 206*)

1½ tablespoons Dijon mustard

1½ tablespoons coarse-grained mustard, such as *moutarde de Meaux*

Salt and pepper

2 veal kidneys, cored and cut into ¼-inch slices

¼ cup oil

1 tablespoon butter

PARSLEY GARNISH:

Reserve 4 small sprigs of the parsley. Bring a large saucepan of salted water to a boil, add all the remaining parsley and the spinach leaves, and boil for 5 minutes. Drain the leaves, refresh them under cold running water, and press lightly to remove excess liquid. Gently pat the cooked leaves between paper towels to dry and set aside.

MUSTARD SAUCE:

In a saucepan set over medium heat, cook 1 tablespoon of the butter until it is brown. Add the shallots and cook them, stirring constantly, for 2 minutes. Increase the heat to medium-high, pour in the cognac, and cook until the liquid has almost evaporated but the shallots are still moist. Then add the chicken stock and continue to cook until reduced by one half, about 5 minutes. Whisk in the *crème fraîche,* cook for 3 minutes, and whisk in the remaining 2 tablespoons of butter. Remove the saucepan from the heat, stir in the mustards, and season to taste with salt and pepper. Keep the sauce warm.

Season the kidney slices with salt and pepper. Set a large frying pan over high heat and add the oil and the 1 tablespoon butter. When the fats are hot, add the kidney slices and sauté them very quickly; the goal is to sear the outsides of the slices while keeping the interiors rosy. Remove the kidney slices to a plate, invert a second plate over the slices to keep warm, and leave them to drain.

To finish the garnish, cook the 2 tablespoons butter in a saucepan over medium heat until the butter is brown. Add the parsley and spinach leaves, season them with salt and pepper, and toss them in the butter until heated through.

Mound portions of the parsley garnish in the centers of 4 plates and arrange the sautéed kidney slices on top of the greens. Pour the mustard sauce in a ribbon around the kidneys and their garnish and set a fresh parsley sprig on each plate.

NOTE: *The parsley garnish is also delicious made with the more readily available curly parsley. This garnish would be an excellent accompaniment to other dishes, too, especially lamb chops or roast chicken. Both the garnish and sauce could be used to good effect with sautéed pork chops in place of the kidneys. Ed.*

Les légumes

VEGETABLES

Purée mousse de haricots verts

Green Bean Purée

To serve 4:

3   pounds green beans
3   tablespoons *crème fraîche* (*page 206*)
3   tablespoons butter
    Salt and pepper

Remove the tips and strings from the beans. Bring a large pot of salted water to a boil. Drop the beans into the boiling water and continue boiling rapidly for 10 minutes. Drain the beans, refresh under cold running water, and drain well. Purée in a food processor or an electric blender, add the *crème fraîche,* and whir again.

❡ **NOTE:** *The recipe can be made ahead to this point. Ed.*

Just before serving, heat the butter in a saucepan over medium low heat until it turns nut brown. Add the purée to the butter, stirring constantly with a wooden spoon until heated through, add salt and pepper as needed, and serve.

Purée mousse de haricots verts minceur

Minceur Green Bean Purée

Make as the preceding recipe, but omit the *crème fraîche* and use only 2 teaspoons butter.

Confiture de légumes de Maman Guérard

Minceur Green Peas and Carrots Braised with Lettuce

To serve 4:

1½	cups shelled young green peas
1	teaspoon olive oil
1	carrot, cut into ¼-inch dice
	Salt and pepper
1	fresh *cèpe* or other fresh mushroom, cut into ¼-inch dice
20	green onions or scallions
2	large hearts of tender green lettuce
½	cup chicken stock (*pages 194–195*)

In a saucepan, boil the peas in salted water for 5 minutes and drain. Heat the olive oil in a flameproof casserole and in it cook the carrot, covered, for 3 minutes without letting it brown. Add a little salt and pepper, the *cèpe,* and the onions. Cook, covered, for 3 minutes.

Then add the peas, cover the vegetables with the lettuce leaves, moisten with the stock, and add salt and pepper again. Braise, covered, over very low heat for 1 hour and 15 minutes. Add water if necessary to keep the level of the liquid in the casserole constant throughout the cooking.

Serve directly from the casserole and wait until the moment of serving to remove the lid.

NOTE: This "marmalade" of vegetables is, in principle, the opposite of cooking them crisp-tender.

Purée mousse de carottes minceur

Minceur Carrot Purée

To serve 4:

1¼ pounds carrots, cut into pieces
    Salt and pepper
2   teaspoons butter

In a saucepan, boil the carrots in salted water for 20 minutes and drain. Purée them in a food processor or an electric blender.

❦ **NOTE:** *The recipe can be prepared ahead to this point. Ed.*

In a saucepan, brown the butter, add the carrot purée, and reheat. Adjust seasoning if necessary and serve. (**NOTE:** *You may use more butter, or add some fresh butter at the end, if you would prefer a gourmande purée. Ed.*)

Gâteau de carottes fondantes au cerfeuil minceur

Minceur Carrot Cake with Chervil

To serve 4:

2   tablespoons butter
1   pound young carrots, thinly sliced
1   cup chicken stock (*pages 194–195*)
    Artificial sweetener equivalent to ½ teaspoon sugar (optional)
    Salt and pepper
1   teaspoon olive oil (optional)

¼ pound mushrooms, finely chopped

1 small shallot, finely chopped

2 eggs

3 tablespoons grated gruyère cheese

2 tablespoons chopped fresh chervil (*see page 212 for substitution*)

Sprigs fresh chervil (for decoration)

Asparagus sauce (*page 202*) or artichoke sauce (*page 202*)

1-pint kugelhopf or ring mold

Heat the butter in a saucepan, add the carrots, and let them brown lightly without becoming soft. Then add the chicken stock, artificial sweetener, and salt and pepper. Simmer the carrots, covered, for 5 minutes. Uncover and cook over moderate heat until the liquid evaporates, about 15 minutes.

Meanwhile, in a nonstick frying pan or a frying pan greased with the 1 teaspoon olive oil, sauté the mushrooms and shallot.

Preheat the oven to 425° F.

Remove the carrots and chop them coarsely. In a bowl, beat the eggs lightly with a fork, add the carrots, mushrooms, gruyère, and chervil, and mix together gently.

Butter the mold very lightly and put in the carrot mixture. Cover the mold with aluminum foil, set it in a baking pan or dish, and add enough water to the pan to come halfway up the mold. Bake in the preheated oven until the carrot mixture is set, 25 to 30 minutes. Unmold onto a platter and pour the sauce around the edge. Decorate the center with sprigs of chervil and serve with a sauceboat of the sauce you have chosen.

Mousse d'épinards aux poires

Spinach Purée with Pear

To serve 4:

1¼   pounds fresh spinach or two 10-ounce
     packages frozen spinach

 1   ripe pear

     Salt and pepper

 3   tablespoons butter

Remove the stems of the fresh spinach and rinse the leaves well. The leaves should weigh about 1 pound. Quarter, peel, and core the pear and cook it gently in plain water until the pieces are tender but not falling apart. Depending on the ripeness of the pear, this may take up to 15 minutes.

Cook the fresh spinach in plenty of boiling salted water for 3 minutes. Drain the spinach, rinse under cold running water, and squeeze out excess water. Cook frozen spinach according to package directions, cutting the cooking time somewhat. Drain but do not rinse, and squeeze out excess water.

Purée the spinach and pear together in a food processor or an electric blender, reheat the purée in a saucepan, simmering it gently if there is too much liquid, and season to taste. Stir in the butter and serve. It is best to make this purée not too long before serving so that it will keep its fresh green color.

Mousse d'épinards aux poires minceur

Minceur Spinach Purée with Pear

Make as the preceding recipe, but omit the butter.

Purée mousse de cresson

Watercress Purée

To serve 4:

2½ quarts tightly packed watercress leaves

2   teaspoons lemon juice

6½ tablespoons butter

½   cup *crème fraîche* (*page 206*)

Salt and pepper

Bring a large pot of salted water to a boil, add the watercress, and boil rapidly for 3 minutes. Drain, refresh under cold running water, and drain thoroughly. Purée the leaves in a food processor or an electric blender.

❮ **NOTE:** *The recipe can be made ahead to this point. Ed.*

Just before serving, put the purée in a saucepan and add the lemon juice, butter, *crème fraîche,* and salt and pepper. Warm the purée slowly over low heat, stirring constantly with a wooden spoon. Serve immediately; the bright color fades quickly after the addition of the lemon juice and cream.

Purée mousse de cresson minceur

Minceur Watercress Purée

Make as the preceding recipe, but omit the butter and reduce the *crème fraîche* to 1 teaspoon.

Purée mousse de céleri

Celeriac Purée

To serve 4:

1   pound celeriac (celery root), peeled and cut
    into 1-inch pieces
1   quart milk
    Salt and pepper
½   cup rice
2   tablespoons *crème fraîche* (*page 206*)

Put the celeriac in a saucepan and add the milk and salt and pepper. Bring to a boil, reduce the heat, and simmer, uncovered, for 10 minutes. Add the rice and continue cooking until the celeriac is tender, about 20 minutes longer. Drain and reserve the liquid.

Put the rice and celeriac in a food processor or an electric blender, add the *crème fraîche,* and purée. Reheat in a saucepan, adding up to ½ cup of the cooking liquid to give the purée a good consistency and salt and pepper as needed. If made ahead of time, reheat over very low heat before serving.

NOTES: Normally potatoes are mixed with celeriac when making a purée, but using rice instead makes the purée equally creamy and also ensures that the flavor of the celeriac comes through clearly. I have made an unusual variation of this recipe with 2 medium apples, peeled, cored, and quartered, instead of rice. They are added 10 minutes before the celeriac is done. The combination of the two tastes is very subtle and absolutely delicious. None of the cooking liquid will be needed for this variation.

Purée mousse de céleri au persil minceur

Minceur Celeriac Purée with Parsley

To serve 4:

1   pound celeriac (celery root), peeled and cut into 1-inch pieces

1   quart milk made with nonfat dry milk and water

Salt and pepper

1   bunch (about ¼ pound) parsley, stems removed

Put the celeriac in a saucepan and add the milk and salt and pepper. Bring to a boil, reduce the heat, and simmer, uncovered, for 20 minutes. Add the parsley and continue cooking until the celeriac is tender, about 10 more minutes. Drain and reserve the liquid.

Put the celeriac and parsley in a food processor or blender and purée, adding the cooking liquid as needed to make a nice smooth purée. Just before serving, reheat and adjust seasoning if necessary.

Ratatouille niçoise minceur

Minceur Ratatouille Niçoise

To serve 4:

3   onions, thinly sliced

1   small green pepper, seeded and cut into ½-inch strips

2   garlic cloves, crushed

¼ pound zucchini, cut into ¼ × ½ × 1 inch
strips

¼ pound piece eggplant, cut as the zucchini

¾ pound tomatoes, peeled, seeded, and cut into
thin wedges

3 tablespoons olive oil

Salt and pepper

Sprig thyme *(see page 212 for substitution)*

½ bay leaf

Preheat the oven to 400° F.

Heat a little of the olive oil in a frying pan and in it sauté the
onions, green pepper, and garlic until they are lightly browned. Remove them from the pan and discard the garlic. Add a little more oil
to the pan, sauté the zucchini and remove it, and then sauté the eggplant in a little more oil.

Combine all the vegetables, including the tomatoes, season to taste
with salt and pepper, put the mixture in a baking dish, and add the
thyme and bay leaf. Bake the ratatouille, uncovered, in the preheated
oven for 30 minutes. After 15 minutes, if the juices in the dish are
reducing too fast, cover with aluminum foil.

Serve warm or at room temperature.

Purée mousse de betteraves au vinaigre

Sweet-and-Sour Beet Purée

To serve 4:

1 teaspoon olive oil

1½ onions, thinly sliced

1 garlic clove, crushed

3 tablespoons red-wine vinegar

¼   cup chopped fresh tomatoes (*page 204*)

8   small (about ¾ pound in all) raw beets, peeled and thinly sliced

    Salt and pepper

1½ tablespoons *crème fraîche* (*page 206*)

6   tablespoons chicken stock (*pages 194–195*)

Heat the olive oil in a large frying pan. Add the onions and garlic and sauté, stirring frequently, until softened but not browned, about 5 minutes.

Stir in the vinegar and then add the tomatoes and sliced beets. Season with salt and pepper, cover, lower the heat, and simmer for 1 hour.

Pour the contents of the pan into a food processor or an electric blender, add the *crème fraîche* and stock, and purée. Just before serving, reheat gently.

NOTE: Although this combination of ingredients might surprise some people, it is delicious, especially when served with game instead of the traditional chestnut purée so common in French restaurants.

Navets "chips"

Turnip Chips

To serve 4:

    Peanut oil (for deep frying)

6   medium-size round turnips

    Salt and pepper

Heat the oil to 375° F. Meanwhile, peel the turnips and cut them into the thinnest slices possible. Pat them dry between paper towels. When the oil is hot, add a quarter of the turnip slices and fry them until golden brown, 2 to 3 minutes. Remove the chips and transfer them to paper towels to drain. Repeat this process until all of the turnip slices have been fried. Season the chips with salt and pepper and serve.

Navets en cocotte au lard

Turnips with Bacon

To serve 4:

6   slices bacon, cut crosswise into ¼-inch strips
6   medium-size round turnips
     Pepper
2   tablespoons olive oil
1   garlic clove, unpeeled

Sauté the bacon strips until most of the fat is rendered and they are lightly browned. Drain them on paper towels and set aside.

Peel the turnips, cut them into ⅛-inch-thick slices, and pepper the slices. Heat the olive oil in a large heavy pan set over high heat. Briskly sauté the turnip slices in the hot oil until lightly browned, turning them from time to time so they color evenly. Turn the heat down to medium-low and add the bacon strips and the garlic clove. Cook the turnips until tender, turning them occasionally, about 10 more minutes. Discard the garlic clove and serve the turnips as an accompaniment to meat or poultry.

Les petits légumes glacés

Glazed Baby Vegetables

To serve 4:

8 baby carrots, with their greens attached *(see* **NOTES***)*

8 baby turnips, with their greens attached *(see* **NOTES***)*

8 green onions or scallions, with their greens attached

3 tablespoons butter

2¼ teaspoons sugar

Salt and pepper

Cut off all but about an inch of the greens and tops from the carrots and turnips. Leave a short stem of green about the same length on each of the onions. Peel the carrots and turnips. Cut the little roots from each onion and remove the first outer skin.

Put the carrots in a frying pan just large enough for them to fit in one layer. Add enough water to barely cover, 1 tablespoon of the butter, ¾ teaspoon of the sugar, and salt and pepper. Bring to a boil, lower the heat, and simmer the carrots, uncovered, for 20 minutes.

Put the turnips and onions in another frying pan; like the carrots, these vegetables should all fit in one layer in the pan with as little space around them as possible. Add enough water to barely cover, the remaining 2 tablespoons butter, 1½ teaspoons sugar, and salt and pepper. Bring to a boil, lower the heat, and simmer, uncovered, for 18 minutes.

The water in both pans will evaporate as the vegetables cook and the butter and sugar will form a syrup. Toward the end of the cooking time, as the syrup forms, shake the pans frequently so that the vegetables will roll in the syrup and be perfectly coated and shiny when ready to serve. Arrange the vegetables on 2 plates and serve at the same time as the main dish they accompany.

NOTES: Baby carrots and turnips with their greens are not always available. Medium-size carrots and turnips can be peeled and cut into olive-shaped pieces and used instead of the baby vegetables. Other vegetables besides those used in this recipe can be cooked the same way provided they are either cut into olive-shaped pieces before cooking or are small vegetables to begin with, such as fresh peas. The vegetables can be slightly browned by continuing the cooking after all the water has evaporated until the syrup begins to caramelize around the cooked vegetables.

Purée mousse de poireaux minceur

Minceur Leek Purée

To serve 4:

5 pounds leeks
6 tablespoons chicken stock (*pages 194–195*)
Salt and pepper
2 teaspoons butter

Cut the white parts of the leeks into thin slices and discard the rest. Rinse the slices well.

In a saucepan, heat the leeks, stirring often, for 5 minutes. Then add the stock and season with salt and pepper. Cook the leeks, uncovered, over low heat until they are very soft, about 30 minutes.

Purée the cooked leeks in a food processor or an electric blender. If the purée is stringy, strain it.

❈ NOTE: *The recipe can be prepared ahead to this point. Ed.*

In a saucepan, brown the 2 teaspoons butter, add the leeks, and reheat. Adjust seasoning if necessary and serve.

Poireaux à l'étuvée

Sautéed Leeks with Cream

To serve 4:

5 pounds leeks
6 tablespoons butter
   Salt and pepper
2 tablespoons *crème fraîche* (*page 206*)

Cut the white part of the leeks into thin slices and discard the rest. Rinse the slices well.

Melt 4 tablespoons of the butter in a frying pan. Add the leeks and cook over medium heat, stirring frequently, for a couple of minutes. Salt and pepper lightly, lower the heat, and continue cooking for 30 minutes, stirring occasionally.

❡ NOTE: *The recipe can be prepared ahead to this point. Ed.*

In a small pan, brown the remaining 2 tablespoons butter. Add it and the *crème fraîche* to the leeks and cook over low heat until hot. Taste for seasoning and adjust if necessary.

Émincé de poireaux minceur à la menthe
sauvage

Minceur Stewed Leeks with Wild Mint

To serve 4:

5   pounds leeks
28 small mint leaves, wild or cultivated
6   tablespoons white wine
    Salt and pepper

Cut the white parts of the leeks into thin slices and discard the rest. Rinse the slices well. Chop 24 of the mint leaves and cut the remaining 4 in fine strips.

In a saucepan, heat the leeks and chopped mint together, stirring often, for 5 minutes. Then add the wine and season with salt and pepper. Cook the leeks, uncovered, over low heat for 30 minutes. Taste for seasoning and adjust as needed. Serve with the strips of mint scattered over the top.

Petites crêpes de maïs

Tiny Corn Crêpes

To serve 4:

¾   cup flour
1   teaspoon salt
    Pinch pepper
1   egg
1   egg yolk

1 cup milk

3½ tablespoons butter

½ cup canned corn kernels, drained

1 tablespoon finely chopped fresh chervil (*see page 212 for substitution*)

Put the flour in a large bowl. Make a well in the center so that the bottom of the bowl is visible. Sprinkle the salt and pepper over the flour, then break the egg into the middle of the well, add the egg yolk, and begin stirring the eggs with a whisk. Pour the milk very slowly into the center of the well, whisking, and gradually incorporate the surrounding flour. Whisk until smooth.

Cook the butter in a small saucepan over medium-low heat until nut brown. Whisk the brown butter into the crêpe batter. Let the batter rest for at least 1 hour.

Just before cooking the crêpes, stir the corn and chervil into the batter. Brush the bottom of a large frying pan with a light coating of oil. Heat the oil over high heat and then add batter to the pan, 1 tablespoon at a time. Each tablespoon of batter will make 1 tiny crêpe. Don't crowd the pan; make as many crêpes as you can at once, but leave enough space between them so that they will not touch when cooking and can be turned over easily. Cook until brown—a matter of seconds—turn over and brown on the other side. Keep the cooked crêpes warm while you finish the rest and then serve immediately.

NOTES: The batter can be made in an electric blender. Simply put the flour, salt, pepper, egg, yolk, milk, and browned butter in the blender and whir until smooth. These crêpes can be served alone as appetizers, or as a vegetable with poultry, and they are especially good with duck and game.

Riz complet

Simple Brown Rice

To serve 4 to 6:

5   tablespoons butter

2   onions, finely chopped

1¼   cups brown rice, rinsed and drained

     Salt and pepper

     Bouquet garni

Preheat the oven to 450° F.

Bring 3½ cups water to a boil. Meanwhile, melt the butter in a heavy flameproof casserole, add the chopped onions, and sauté over medium heat until soft but not brown, about 5 minutes. Increase the heat to high and add the drained rice, the boiling water, salt and pepper, and the bouquet garni. Stir well. When the water returns to a boil, cover the casserole and bake the rice in the preheated oven until all the water has been absorbed, about 1 hour. Remove the bouquet garni and serve directly from the casserole.

Pommes à la peau

Unpeeled Potato Slices

To serve 4:

4   large potatoes (about 1¾ pounds in all), unpeeled

     Salt and pepper

6   tablespoons butter

Put the potatoes in a pot of salted water, bring to a boil, and cook for 30 minutes. Drain the potatoes and let cool for several minutes. Cut the potatoes into slices a little more than ¼ inch thick and season the slices on both sides with salt and pepper.

Heat the butter in a large frying pan over high heat and add as many potato slices as will fit in one layer. Fry about 2 minutes on each side. Keep warm while frying the rest of the potatoes and then serve immediately.

NOTE: The potato skins brown in the hot butter and give the potatoes a fresh, almost fruity taste.

Purée de pommes de terre au persil

Mashed Potatoes with Parsley

To serve 4:

1¾	pounds floury potatoes
1⅔	cups milk
6	tablespoons butter, softened
¼	cup finely chopped parsley
	Salt

Peel the potatoes and cut them into quarters. Put them in a pot with cold water and salt. Bring to a boil over high heat, cover, lower the heat, and boil slowly for 20 minutes. The potatoes should not be overcooked.

Bring the milk to a boil in a small saucepan and keep warm over very low heat.

Drain the potatoes and put them back into the pot they were cooked in. Mash the potatoes with a fork, adding the butter as you do so. The potatoes are deliberately left a bit lumpy. Put the pot over medium heat and slowly add the boiled milk, stirring constantly with a wooden spoon. The potatoes will become creamier and lighter. Stir in the parsley and salt if needed and serve immediately.

Pommes sautées à cru en persillade

Sautéed Potatoes with Parsley

To serve 4:

2	pounds potatoes
⅔	cup peanut oil
6	tablespoons butter
	Salt and pepper
1	tablespoon chopped parsley

Peel the potatoes, cut into slices ⅛ inch thick, and wash the slices under cold running water. Drain well and then dry the slices on paper towels.

In a very large frying pan or 2 smaller ones, heat the peanut oil over high heat. Add the potato slices and sauté, turning them from time to time, until they are golden, about 10 minutes.

In another large frying pan, heat the butter over medium heat. With a slotted spoon, transfer the potatoes to the hot butter. Cook the potato slices in the butter, turning them occasionally, until they are tender, about 5 minutes. Season the potatoes with salt and pepper. Transfer the sautéed potatoes to a serving plate, sprinkle with the chopped parsley, and serve.

Pommes mitron

Braised Potatoes and Onions

To serve 4:

1½	pounds potatoes
6	tablespoons butter
1	tablespoon peanut oil
	Salt and pepper
1	onion, halved lengthwise and thinly sliced
1	garlic clove, finely chopped
	Sprig thyme (or ½ teaspoon dried thyme)
2	cups chicken stock (*pages 194–195*)

Peel the potatoes and cut into slices ⅛ inch thick. Rinse the slices in cold water, drain, and pat them dry between paper towels.

Preheat the oven to 475° F.

In a large frying pan, heat 2 tablespoons of the butter with the peanut oil and add half of the potatoes. Cook them over medium heat until slightly softened but not browned, about 5 minutes. Give the pan a good shake every now and then to prevent the potatoes from sticking. Season them with salt and pepper and remove them from the pan. Cook the remaining potatoes in the same way.

Add 2 more tablespoons of the butter to the pan and cook the onion over medium-high heat until lightly browned, stirring frequently to prevent it from scorching, about 7 minutes. Season with salt and pepper.

Put half of the potato slices in a baking dish or casserole. Cover with the sautéed onion. Sprinkle the chopped garlic over the onion and top with the remaining potato slices. Add the sprig of thyme. Pour the chicken stock over the layered vegetables—it should just cover them. Cut the remaining 2 tablespoons butter into small pieces and distribute evenly over the surface. Bake the potatoes in the preheated oven until tender, about 45 minutes. Serve directly from the baking dish or casserole.

Mon gratin dauphinois

Potato Gratin Michel Guérard

To serve 4:

1¾   pounds potatoes

1   teaspoon salt

    Pinch pepper

1   cup milk

1   cup *crème fraîche* (*page 206*)

½   garlic clove, finely chopped

    Nutmeg

2   tablespoons butter

4 round baking dishes, about 5 inches in diameter

Peel the potatoes and cut them into slices ⅛ inch thick. Do not wash the potato slices but pat them dry with paper towels. Using your hands, rub the potatoes well with the salt and pepper.

Preheat the oven to 450° F.

Pour the milk into a saucepan, add the potatoes, and bring to a boil. Lower the heat, cover the pan, and simmer for 10 minutes. Add the *crème fraîche,* garlic, and a grating of nutmeg. Continue cooking slowly, covered, for 20 minutes longer. While the potatoes are cooking, stir them occasionally to prevent them from sticking to the bottom of the pan; be careful not to crush or break them.

Once they are cooked, lift the potatoes out of the pot with a slotted spoon and put them in the individual baking dishes. Pour enough of the cooking liquid into each dish to cover the slices. Dot the surfaces with the butter. Put the baking dishes in a large roasting pan and add enough water to the pan to come halfway up the sides of the dishes. Put the pan in the preheated oven and bake until the potatoes begin to brown, about 10 minutes. Serve immediately.

NOTES: I don't know why, but potatoes cooked this way always have a pleasant cheeselike taste. Could it come from the starch in the potatoes combining with the cream? Anyway, it is essential not to wash the potatoes before cooking them. This way the starch on each slice is left intact and helps thicken the cream-milk mixture during cooking. Prepared just this way, the potatoes are delicious, but for those who can't resist the temptation, a little grated cheese can be sprinkled over them just before they go into the oven.

Pommes de terre vapeur au lard et au thym

Steamed Potatoes with Bacon and Thyme

To serve 4:

4   large potatoes (about 1¾ pounds in all), unpeeled

Salt and pepper

4   slices bacon, each slice cut in half

½   teaspoon thyme or, preferably, thyme flowers

Split the potatoes in half lengthwise and scoop out enough pulp from each half potato to make a shallow indentation. Salt the potatoes lightly and then put a half slice of bacon on each half. Sprinkle the bacon with thyme and a little pepper.

Steam the potatoes, bacon side up, over boiling water (*see* **NOTE** *page 113*) until soft, about 30 minutes. Sprinkle with salt and pepper and serve.

NOTES: During steaming some of the fat in the bacon will melt into the potatoes and spread its flavor as well as that of the thyme through the pulp. Potatoes steamed in this way can be turned into a main dish by simply adding sausages to the steamer with the potatoes and cooking them all together. This makes for a hearty, country-style meal.

Les nouilles au citron

Noodles in Lemon Sauce

To serve 4 to 6:

3	tablespoons cold butter
	Grated zest of 1 lemon
2	tablespoons white wine
2	tablespoons *crème fraîche* (*page 206*)
1	teaspoon lemon juice
½	pound fresh or frozen noodles
	Salt and pepper
1	tablespoon grated parmesan cheese

Bring a large pot of salted water to a boil.

LEMON SAUCE:

Melt 1 tablespoon of the butter in a small saucepan, add the grated lemon zest, and cook over low heat for 3 minutes. Increase the heat, add the white wine, and cook until it has reduced by one half. Then whisk in the *crème fraîche*, the remaining 2 tablespoons butter, and the lemon juice and remove the saucepan from the heat. The sauce should be smooth and creamy.

When the water boils, add the noodles and cook them until just tender, 5 to 10 minutes. Drain the noodles and transfer them to a serving bowl. Pour the sauce over the noodles and season with salt and pepper. Gently toss the noodles to coat them evenly with the sauce. Sprinkle with the grated parmesan and serve immediately.

Les desserts

DESSERTS

Fruits au vin de graves rouge

Fresh Fruit in Red Wine

To serve 4:

1¼	cups red Bordeaux wine, preferably a Graves
3	tablespoons sugar
1	vanilla bean, split lengthwise
1	pound assorted fruit *(see* **NOTE***)*
8	small fresh mint leaves

NOTE: *Suggested fruits are oranges, berries, cherries, grapes, pears, peaches, and melon. Choose three or four. Ed.*

In a saucepan, boil the wine until it is reduced by one half. Add ½ cup water, the sugar, and split vanilla bean and bring the mixture back to a boil. Let it cool and then refrigerate.

Over a bowl to catch their juices, peel the larger fruits, core or pit them, and cut them into half-moon slices or sections. Leave the berries and grapes whole; pit cherries or not as you prefer. Chill the whole combination in the fruit juices for at least 1 hour.

To serve, spoon the fruit into chilled wine glasses, pour the sweetened wine over them, and decorate with the vanilla bean, cut into quarters, and the mint leaves.

Fruits au vin de graves rouge minceur

Minceur Fresh Fruit in Red Wine

Make as the preceding recipe, but use artificial sweetener equivalent to 3 tablespoons of sugar or simply use less real sugar.

Oranges aux zestes

Oranges with Candied Zest

To serve 4:

4   large blood or navel oranges

1   cup sugar

4   kiwis

    Strawberry, raspberry, or black currant
    sauce (*page 209*)

Pare off in strips all the zest from 2 of the oranges. Cut the strips into thin shreds. In a saucepan, bring 2 cups of water and the sugar to a boil, add the orange zest, and simmer over very low heat until candied, about 1 hour.

With a sharp knife, peel all the oranges completely, down to the flesh. Over a bowl to catch the juice, cut the sections out from between the membranes. Peel the kiwis and cut them crosswise into thin slices.

To serve, arrange the orange sections in pinwheels on individual plates and the kiwi slices in a ring around them. Sprinkle the candied zest over the oranges and spoon the reserved orange juice over them. Spoon the sauce over all and serve.

Oranges aux zestes minceur

Minceur Oranges with Candied Zest

Make as the preceding recipe, but substitute artificial sweetener equivalent to 1 cup of sugar and use minceur strawberry, raspberry, or black currant sauce (*page 209*).

Fruits frais à la gelée d'amande minceur

Minceur Fresh Fruit with Almond Jelly

To serve 4:

ALMOND JELLY:

1½ teaspoons gelatine

½ cup milk made with nonfat dry milk and water

Scant ½ teaspoon almond extract

8 or 9 fresh fruits *(see* **NOTE***)*

4 small sprigs mint

Shallow round mold, 7 inches in diameter

NOTE: *Choose seasonal fruits in as much variety as possible, for instance an orange, a grapefruit, a tangerine, berries, grapes, a kiwi, a pear, a pineapple. Only a few pieces of each fruit are used per serving. Ed.*

ALMOND JELLY:

Soak the gelatine in a spoonful of cold water until it is soft. Bring the milk to a boil, remove from the heat, and immediately add the softened gelatine and the almond extract. Stir until the gelatine has dissolved completely. Pour into the mold; the mixture should be ⅜ inch deep. Refrigerate to set.

Leave small fruits whole and cut or section larger ones into attractive pieces. Prepare the fruits over a bowl to collect their juices and let them all macerate together in the refrigerator.

With a knife or cookie cutter, cut the almond jelly into lozenges, squares, or circles as you prefer. Lift them out with a metal spatula, arrange them in the centers of chilled plates, and decorate with the mint sprigs. Arrange the fruit decoratively around the almond jelly and spoon the fruit juice over the fruit. Serve immediately while everything is still chilled.

Pommes bonne femme à l'amande d'abricot

Baked Apples with Almond-Apricot Filling

To serve 4:

8 almonds, skinned and split in half

4 dried apricots, cut into ¼-inch dice

3 tablespoons sugar

2 tablespoons rum

4 large apples, stems intact

3 tablespoons butter

Apricot sauce *(page 210)*

Put the almonds in a bowl with the apricots, 1 teaspoon of the sugar, and the rum and let macerate for 1 hour.

Preheat the oven to 425° F.

Peel the apples, but do not remove their stems. Cut off the top of each apple just under the stem and reserve. Use an apple corer or small knife to remove the seeds but don't pierce the bottoms of the apples. Fill each apple with the almond-apricot mixture, put the apples in a baking dish, and pour any excess rum over them. Put 1 heaping teaspoon of butter on top of each apple and cover each one with its top. Sprinkle each apple with a teaspoon of sugar and add ½ cup water and 4 teaspoons of the butter to the baking dish. Bake in the preheated oven until the apples are cooked through but not too soft or mushy, 30 to 40 minutes. Halfway through the cooking time, baste the apples with the liquid in the baking dish and sprinkle each one once more with a teaspoon of sugar.

Just before the apples are ready to come from the oven, warm the apricot sauce. Serve either in the baking dish with the apricot sauce poured over the apples or spoon apricot sauce onto 4 plates, place the apples on the plates, and spoon the juice from the baking dish over them.

NOTE: Fresh fruits can be used instead of the dried apricots and almonds for the filling, such as pitted cherries, strawberries, or raspberries. If fresh fruit is used, accompany the apples with raspberry sauce (*page 209*) rather than apricot sauce. This dessert is delicious served cold, especially in the summertime.

Bananes en papillote minceur

Minceur Bananas Baked in Foil

To serve 4:

Artificial sweetener equivalent to 3 tablespoons sugar

Minceur apricot sauce *(page 210)*

Scant ¼ teaspoon almond extract

4   small ripe bananas, peeled

2   vanilla beans, split lengthwise

4   sprigs fresh mint (optional)

Four 12 × 8 inch pieces aluminum foil

Preheat the oven to 425° F.

·Bring ¼ cup water to a boil in a small saucepan and stir in the artificial sweetener. Remove from the heat, add the apricot sauce and the almond extract, and whisk well.

Put a banana on each piece of foil and turn up the edges to hold the sauce. Pour the apricot sauce over the bananas and add the split vanilla beans. Close the foil by folding over the edges and pinching them together securely. Place on a baking sheet.

Bake the bananas in the preheated oven for 15 minutes. Serve on plates in the unopened foil packages or open the foil first and decorate the bananas with sprigs of fresh mint.

NOTE: The same recipe can be used to make apples en papillote.

Granité au vin de Saint-Émilion

Bordeaux Ice

To serve 6 to 8:

1	cup sugar
1	bottle red Bordeaux wine, preferably a Saint-Émilion
	Juice of 1 orange
	Juice of 1 lemon
6 to 8	fresh mint leaves (optional)

Put one cup of water and the sugar in a saucepan, bring to a boil, and boil for 1 minute. Pour the syrup into a bowl and let cool completely.

Once the syrup has cooled, stir in the wine, orange juice, and lemon juice. Pour the mixture into a shallow metal pan and freeze, stirring the mixture well with a fork every hour, for 5 to 6 hours.

❦ **NOTE:** *This ice can be made ahead, but since it will harden completely, it must be removed from the freezer and left in the refrigerator to soften for 20 minutes before mixing once more, to break up the ice crystals, and serving. Ed.*

To serve, fill stemmed wine glasses with the ice, stick a fresh mint leaf into each portion, and serve immediately.

NOTES: The orange juice can be replaced by fresh tangerine juice, creating an unusual combination full of flavor. Another delicious variation of this recipe can be made using very small fresh peaches. Peel the peaches but do not remove the pits. Put the peaches in a saucepan with a syrup made by boiling 4 cups of water with 2⅔ cups of sugar. Add a vanilla bean split open lengthwise and poach the fruit for 15 minutes. Cool completely. Once the glasses have been filled with the ice, place a peach on the ice in each glass and put a mint leaf where the stem of the peach was.

Ananas glacé

Pineapple Ice Boats

To serve 6:

One 3-pound pineapple

¾ cup sugar

3 tablespoons lemon juice

2 tablespoons kirsch

Fresh strawberries (for garnish, optional)

Set the pineapple on its side and cut it in half lengthwise, slicing through both fruit and crown. With a small knife and a spoon, remove as much of the pineapple flesh as is possible, keeping the shells intact. Discard the tough, fibrous core and put the remaining flesh in an electric blender or a food processor. Put the hollowed-out pineapple shells into the freezer.

Add the sugar, lemon juice, and kirsch to the blender or processor and blend until smooth. Pour this mixture into a shallow metal pan and freeze until set but not hard, about 1 hour and 30 minutes. Scoop this ice into the frozen pineapple shells and return them to the freezer.

❰ **NOTE:** *If the pineapple shells have been filled more than 2 hours ahead of time, transfer them to the refrigerator 20 minutes before serving so the ice isn't rock-hard. Ed.*

To serve, arrange the filled pineapple shells on a serving platter and garnish, if you like, with fresh strawberries.

Sorbet au chocolat amer et sa salade d'oranges

Bitter Chocolate Sherbet with Oranges

To serve 4 to 6:

2	cups coffee
2½	ounces unsweetened chocolate, grated
½	cup sugar
5	oranges

In a saucepan, heat the coffee with the grated chocolate and the sugar. Stir well. When the chocolate and sugar have melted and the mixture is smooth, pour it into a shallow metal baking pan and freeze until firm, about 3 hours.

Break the frozen mixture into chunks and whir in a food processor until the mixture lightens in color and becomes smooth. Working quickly so the sherbet doesn't melt, pack it into a storage container and return to the freezer until firm, at least 1 hour.

With a sharp knife, peel the oranges. Be sure to remove all of the bitter white pith that adheres to the fruit. Once the oranges are peeled, slice in between the membranes to remove the orange sections.

❰ **NOTE:** *The recipe can be made ahead and simply assembled at the last moment, or the sherbet mixture can be made and frozen one day and processed* *and refrozen the next. If you keep the sherbet for several days and it becomes crystallized during storage, simply process again and refreeze. Ed.*

To serve, scoop the sherbet into chilled parfait glasses and garnish with the orange sections.

Poires en sabayon de rhum blanc

Pear Gratins with Rum Sabayon

To serve 4:

POACHED PEARS:

1	quart water
1	cup sugar
4	firm pears with stems
2	tablespoons lemon juice
1	teaspoon finely chopped lemon zest
1	teaspoon finely chopped orange zest

RUM SABAYON:

3	egg yolks
¼	cup pear cooking liquid, above
3½	tablespoons white rum

4 individual gratin dishes

POACHED PEARS:

In a large saucepan, bring the water to a boil with the sugar. Peel the pears and core from the bottom, scooping out all the seeds but leaving the stems intact. Trim the bottoms, if necessary, so they'll stand upright and rub the pears with the lemon juice to prevent them from discoloring. Put them in the hot syrup and poach them, uncovered, until softened, 15 minutes or longer depending on the type of pear and degree of ripeness. Remove the saucepan from the heat and let the pears cool in their syrup.

Blanch the lemon and orange zests in a small saucepan of boiling water for 5 minutes. Drain, rinse under cold running water, and drain well.

❦ **NOTE:** *The recipe can be prepared ahead to this point. Ed.*

Preheat the oven to 475° F.

RUM SABAYON:

In a heavy-based saucepan, whisk together the egg yolks, pear cooking liquid, and the rum. Set the saucepan over the lowest possible heat and continue whisking briskly just until the mixture lightens in color and becomes creamy. Remove from the heat.

Drain the pears and put 1 in each gratin dish. Cover the pears with the sabayon and sprinkle with the blanched zests. Bake in the preheated oven until the sabayon has browned nicely, about 7 minutes, and serve immediately.

Gratin de fruits frais

Fresh Fruit Gratins

To serve 4:

1   pound fresh fruit *(see* **NOTE***)*
4   egg yolks
¼   cup granulated sugar or 6 tablespoons
     powdered sugar

1   tablespoon *crème fraîche (page 206)*

1   tablespoon rum

4 individual gratin dishes

NOTE: *Almost any soft fruit can be used in this recipe and in as much or as little variety as you like. Suggestions are: oranges, grapefruit, berries, cherries, grapes, kiwis, pears, and peaches. Citrus fruits should be peeled down to the flesh with a knife and then sliced in between the membranes to free the flesh in segments. Strawberries should be hulled, cherries pitted, grapes seeded if necessary, and kiwis peeled. Pears and peaches should be peeled and cored or pitted. Berries, grapes, and cherries can be used whole. Larger fruits, once peeled and cored or pitted, should be cut into pieces. Ed.*

Preheat the oven to 475° F.

Prepare the fruits you have chosen and arrange them in the gratin dishes.

In a heavy-based saucepan, whisk together the egg yolks, sugar, and 2 tablespoons water. Set the saucepan over the lowest possible heat and continue whisking vigorously until the mixture lightens in color and becomes creamy. Remove the saucepan from the heat, whisk in the *crème fraîche* and rum, and pour over the fruit. Set the gratins on a baking sheet and bake them in the preheated oven until the surfaces are very lightly browned, about 7 minutes. Serve immediately.

Soufflé aux framboises

Raspberry Soufflés

To serve 6:

1   tablespoon butter, melted

⅓   cup granulated sugar

1   pint fresh or ½ pound frozen raspberries

2   tablespoons lemon juice

2   egg yolks

8   egg whites
     Pinch salt

¼   cup powdered sugar

1½   recipes raspberry sauce *(page 209)* (optional)

*6 individual soufflé molds, 4 inches in diameter
and 2 inches deep*

Preheat the oven to 425° F.

Lightly butter the inside of each soufflé mold, using the melted butter and a pastry brush. Use 4 teaspoons of the granulated sugar to coat the molds, turning them so that the sides and bottoms are coated with a thin layer of sugar, as though you were flouring them. Turn the mold upside down so that any excess sugar will fall out.

Put the raspberries, lemon juice, and the remaining ¼ cup of granulated sugar in a food processor or an electric blender and purée. Add the egg yolks and whir briefly. Pour the mixture into a large bowl.

Put the egg whites and a pinch of salt in a second large bowl and beat or whisk to the soft-peak stage. Sprinkle in the powdered sugar and continue beating just long enough to mix the sugar into the egg whites.

Using a spatula, carefully fold the egg whites into the fruit purée, a quarter at a time. Spoon the soufflé mixture into the prepared molds and sweep off any excess with a flexible-blade spatula or a knife so the top of each is level with the rim. Run your thumb around the interior edge of the rim to make a small groove. Put the soufflés on a baking sheet and bake in the preheated oven for 12 minutes. Set on plates and serve immediately either plain or accompanied by a sauceboat of raspberry sauce.

NOTES: Buttering the molds is essential since it permits the soufflés to rise straight up when baking. The sugar gives the outside of the soufflés a hint of crispness that is quite pleasant. Be careful not to touch the inside of the molds once they have been buttered and sugared. The soufflés can be glazed by sprinkling a little powdered sugar over the top of each soufflé 3 minutes after it goes into the oven.

Crème brulée aux framboises

Raspberry Crème Brulée

To serve 4 to 6:

1   cup *crème fraîche (page 206)*
6   egg yolks
1   cup granulated sugar
2   pints fresh or 1 pound frozen raspberries
4   tablespoons brown sugar

4 to 6 individual ramekins (see **NOTE***)*

Bring the *crème fraîche* to a boil in a medium-size saucepan. In a large bowl, whisk the egg yolks with the sugar until the mixture lightens in color and becomes creamy. Whisk in the scalded *crème fraîche* and then pour the mixture back into the saucepan. Cook over low heat, stirring continuously with a wooden spoon until the custard is thick enough to coat the spoon, about 10 minutes.

Divide the raspberries among the ramekins. Cover them with the custard and refrigerate until the custard is cold and firm.

❪ **NOTE:** *The recipe can be prepared ahead to this point. Ed.*

Preheat the broiler.

Set the ramekins on a baking sheet and sprinkle a thin layer of brown sugar over the surface of each one. Broil until the sugar has caramelized, about 2 minutes. Set the ramekins on plates and serve immediately.

NOTE: This dessert could also be prepared in a single large baking dish.

Poire rôtie au four et son gratin d'amandes

Caramelized Poached Pears with Almond Gratin

To serve 4:

POACHED PEARS:

1 quart water

1 cup granulated sugar

4 firm pears

2 tablespoons lemon juice

ALMOND GRATIN:

Zest of 1 orange, finely chopped

Zest of 2 lemons, finely chopped

5½ tablespoons butter, softened

¾ cup powdered sugar

¾ cup ground blanched almonds

2 eggs

1 tablespoon rum

1½ tablespoons granulated sugar

2 teaspoons butter

4   mint leaves
1   cup black currant syrup, in a sauceboat *(see*
     NOTE*)*

Small gratin dish

NOTE: *Nonalcoholic black currant syrup is generally available in liquor stores and specialty food shops. Ed.*

POACHED PEARS:

In a large saucepan, bring the water to a boil with the sugar. Peel, halve, and core the pears and rub them with the lemon juice to prevent discoloring. Put them in the hot syrup and poach, uncovered, until softened, 10 minutes or longer depending on the type of pear and degree of ripeness. Remove the pan from the heat and let the pears cool in their syrup.

ALMOND GRATIN:

Bring a small saucepan of water to a boil, add the orange and lemon zests, and blanch them for 5 minutes. Drain the zests, rinse under cold running water, and drain well. In a bowl, cream the softened butter with the powdered sugar and the ground almonds. Add the eggs, the rum, and the chopped zests and mix well. *(***NOTE:*** The gratin can also be made in a food processor. In this case, you can start with slivered or sliced blanched almonds, and the zests needn't be chopped. Process the zests, almonds, and powdered sugar first. Add the butter and whir again, and then the eggs and rum and process once more until combined. Ed.)* Pour this mixture into a small gratin dish.\

❡ **NOTE:** *The recipe can be prepared ahead to this point. Ed.*

Preheat the broiler.
Drain the pears and reserve the syrup. Arrange the pears, cut side down, in a baking dish large enough to hold them in one layer. Sprinkle them with the 1½ tablespoons sugar, spoon 6 tablespoons of the reserved syrup over the pears, and dot them with the 2 teaspoons of butter.

Broil the almond mixture until its surface is lightly browned, about 3 minutes, and then transfer it to the oven. Broil the pears until they are lightly caramelized, about 5 minutes. Arrange the pear halves on 4 individual plates, garnish each plate with a mint leaf, and serve, accompanied by the sauceboat of black currant syrup and the hot almond gratin.

Soufflé glacé au chocolat amer

Frozen Bitter Chocolate Soufflé

To serve 8:

3	tablespoons instant coffee
¼	cup rum
1	cup unsweetened Dutch cocoa
¾	cup granulated sugar
6	eggs, separated
2	cups heavy cream
2	tablespoons powdered sugar
1	teaspoon vanilla extract
	Pinch salt

6-cup soufflé dish

Wrap a double layer of parchment paper or aluminum foil around the soufflé dish to form a collar that extends at least 3 inches above the rim of the dish. Tie a piece of string around the collar to keep it in place.

In a small bowl, dissolve the instant coffee in the rum and 2 tablespoons of water. Add the cocoa and stir well until it is smooth. You will have a stiff paste.

In a small saucepan set over medium-high heat, combine ½ cup of the granulated sugar with 2 tablespoons of water and cook until the sugar is completely dissolved. In a medium-size bowl, beat the egg yolks until they have lightened in color and thickened slightly. With an electric mixer, beat the hot syrup into the beaten yolks and continue beating until the mixture has cooled completely. Add the coffee-cocoa mixture and beat until smooth.

❡ **NOTE:** *The recipe can be prepared ahead to this point. Ed.*

Whip the cream with the powdered sugar and the vanilla. Beat the egg whites with the salt until they hold stiff peaks. Then beat in the remaining ¼ cup sugar, beating until the peaks are stiff and satiny. Gently fold together the beaten whites, the whipped cream, and the chocolate mixture.

Spoon the soufflé mixture into the prepared dish and freeze it for 3 to 4 hours. It will be firm on the outside and creamy in the center. For a completely frozen soufflé, freeze it overnight.

To serve, remove the paper collar. At the table, cut the soufflé in quarters down to the rim of the dish. Slice the soufflé off at rim height, making 4 portions. Put these on individual plates, then cut the remaining soufflé in quarters, and transfer to plates.

Tarte fine aux pommes chaudes minceur

Minceur Hot Apple Tarts

To serve 4:

PASTRY (PÂTE BRISÉE):

⅞   cup flour

6   tablespoons cold butter, cut into small pieces
    Pinch salt

3   crisp, tart apples

½   recipe minceur apricot sauce *(page 210)*

PASTRY:

Sift the flour. Put the butter in an electric blender and add the flour, salt, and 1 tablespoon water. Blend briefly, until the mixture is mealy; you will need to stop the blender at least once to push down the flour with a rubber spatula. Turn the mixture out onto a piece of waxed paper, gather it together in one mass, and press this dough together firmly into a ball.

Put the ball of dough on a floured work surface and knead it quickly with the heel of your hand until you have a homogeneous dough; do not let it get sticky. Gather it together in a smooth round ball, flatten this somewhat, cover it well, and refrigerate for at least 30 minutes.

Divide the dough into 4 equal pieces, roll them into balls, and flour them lightly. Roll them out on a lightly floured surface into very thin, 5-inch rounds. Using a small plate or pan lid as a guide, trim the pieces of pastry into perfect circles. With a spatula, transfer them to a baking sheet.

❰ NOTE: *The recipe can be prepared ahead to this point. Cover the pastry and refrigerate. Ed.*

Preheat the oven to 425° F.

Peel and core the apples and cut them into very thin half-moon slices. Arrange the slices pinwheel-style on the pastry, covering it completely. Bake the tarts in the preheated oven for 20 minutes. Meanwhile, warm the apricot sauce. Remove the tarts from the oven and paint them with the warm sauce. Transfer the tarts to individual plates and serve immediately.

Feuilleté de pommes normandes et son sabayon au calvados

Norman Apple Pastries with Calvados Sabayon

To serve 4:

1	pound puff pastry *(page 207)*
½	egg, beaten
1	teaspoon powdered sugar

FILLING:

4	Golden Delicious apples
2	tablespoons butter
16	canned apricot halves in syrup
2	tablespoons granulated sugar
1	teaspoon vanilla extract

SABAYON:

3	egg yolks
¼	cup apricot syrup, from above
3½	tablespoons calvados or applejack

Preheat the oven to 425° F.

On a lightly floured work surface, roll out the puff pastry to a square ¼ inch thick and at least 11 inches on a side. Using a small plate or pan lid that is 4 to 5 inches in diameter as a guide, cut out 4 pastry circles, turn them over, and transfer to a baking sheet lightly sprinkled with water. Brush the tops with the beaten egg. With the tip of a sharp knife, score the surfaces lightly in a diamond pattern. Cook the pastries in the preheated oven until puffed and browned, 25 to 30 minutes. Sprinkle the tops with the powdered sugar and return the pastries to the oven to caramelize the surfaces, about 2 minutes. Keep the pastries warm in the turned-off oven.

FILLING:

Peel and core the apples and cut into ½-inch cubes. Melt the butter in a frying pan, add the cubed apples, and sauté over moderately high heat until softened, about 8 minutes. Drain the apricots, reserving the syrup, and stir them, the granulated sugar, and the vanilla extract into the apples. Keep the fruit warm.

❡ **NOTE:** *The recipe can be prepared ahead to this point. Reheat the fruit and the pastry when ready to serve. Ed.*

SABAYON:

In a heavy-based saucepan, whisk together the egg yolks, ¼ cup of the reserved apricot syrup, and the calvados. Set the saucepan over the lowest possible heat and continue whisking briskly just until the mixture lightens in color and becomes creamy. Remove from the heat.

Cut the warm pastries in half horizontally with a serrated knife and put the bottoms on individual plates or on a serving platter. Spoon the filling onto the pastries and cover with the tops. Pour the sabayon around the pastries and serve immediately.

Crêpes à la paresseuse

Crêpes with Almond Butter

To serve 4:

CRÊPES:

1	egg
1	egg yolk
⅔	cup flour
2	tablespoons sugar
¾	cup milk
	Zest of ½ orange, finely grated
3	tablespoons butter

ALMOND BUTTER:

¼	cup sugar
½	cup shelled almonds
¼	pound butter, softened
1	tablespoon orange liqueur

8	teaspoons armagnac or cognac

7-inch crêpe pan or small frying pan

CRÊPES:

Make the crêpe batter and cook the crêpes as for cheese soufflé crêpes (*pages 42–43*), substituting the 2 tablespoons sugar for the salt and the grated orange zest for the herbs.

ALMOND BUTTER:

Butter a baking sheet lightly. Put the sugar, 1 tablespoon water, and the almonds in a small pan. Set it over medium heat and cook, stirring with a wooden spoon, until it turns a dark caramel color. Immediately pour the mixture onto the prepared baking sheet and leave to cool completely. It should become very hard. Break this almond brittle (*pralin*) into pieces and grind to a coarse powder in a food processor or heavy-duty blender. Add the ¼ pound butter and the orange liqueur and whir until well combined.

❡ **NOTE:** *The recipe can be prepared ahead to this point. Ed.*

Preheat the oven to 475° F.

Spread one side of each crêpe with a thin layer of the almond butter.

Lightly butter 8 dessert plates. Place each crêpe on its own small plate, almond-butter side up. Put the plates in the preheated oven for just 30 seconds. Remove from the oven, sprinkle each crêpe with a teaspoon of armagnac, and serve immediately. Each person is served 2 crêpes, each on its own plate.

Crêpes gratinées aux pommes

Apple Crêpes Baked with Almond Cream

To serve 4:

CRÊPES:

1   egg

1   egg yolk

⅔   cup flour

2   tablespoons granulated sugar

¾   cup milk

3   tablespoons butter

APPLE FILLING:

3   apples

4   tablespoons butter

6   canned apricot halves, drained

2   teaspoons vanilla extract

½   cup granulated sugar

ALMOND CREAM:

4   tablespoons butter, softened

½   cup powdered sugar

½   cup finely ground blanched almonds

1   egg

1   tablespoon rum

½   cup sliced almonds

⅓   cup calvados or applejack

Make the crêpe batter and cook the crêpes as for cheese soufflé crêpes (*pages 42–43*), substituting the 2 tablespoons sugar for the salt and omitting the parsley and tarragon.

APPLE FILLING:

Peel and core the apples and cut them into large dice. In a large frying pan (nonstick, if possible), cook the butter over medium-high heat until it is brown. Add the apples and the apricots and sauté them until browned, about 10 minutes. Stir in the vanilla and the ½ cup sugar and cook, stirring, until the sugar begins to caramelize, about 1 minute. Remove from the heat and set aside.

ALMOND CREAM:

Cream the softened butter and gradually add the powdered sugar and the ground almonds. Blend in the egg and mix well for 2 minutes. Stir in the rum. (**NOTE:** *This can be done in a food processor. Process the* *almonds, which can be sliced or slivered rather than ground, with the sugar. Add the butter and whir again. Then add the egg and rum and process once more until combined. Ed.)*

❲ **NOTE:** *The recipe can be prepared ahead to this point. Ed.*

Preheat the oven to 400° F.

Butter a shallow baking dish large enough to accommodate the crêpes in a single layer. Spoon some of the fruit filling near one edge of each crêpe. Roll the crêpes around the filling to form cylinders and place them, flap side down, in the buttered baking dish. Spread the almond cream over the crêpes and sprinkle with the sliced almonds. Bake in the preheated oven until lightly browned, about 10 minutes. Sprinkle the calvados over the surface and serve immediately.

Poires belle-Hélène

Pears with Vanilla Ice Cream and Warm Chocolate Sauce

To serve 4:

POACHED PEARS:

1   quart water

1   cup granulated sugar

4   firm pears with stems

2   tablespoons lemon juice

Four ½-inch-thick slices brioche or other rich egg bread

⅔   cup sliced almonds

2   tablespoons powdered sugar

CHOCOLATE SAUCE:

¾ cup unsweetened Dutch cocoa

1 cup granulated sugar

2 tablespoons butter

½ pint vanilla ice cream, slightly softened

8 fresh verbena or mint leaves

Poach the pears as described in pear gratins with rum sabayon (*page 172*).

Preheat the oven to 425° F.

Put the slices of brioche on a baking sheet and sprinkle them with the sliced almonds and the powdered sugar. Toast them in the preheated oven until the almonds are lightly browned, about 5 minutes. Transfer the slices to a serving platter or to individual plates.

CHOCOLATE SAUCE:

In a saucepan, combine the cocoa, sugar, and 1 cup water and whisk until smooth. Set the saucepan over high heat and bring to a boil. Lower heat and simmer the sauce, whisking, for 3 minutes, add the butter, and simmer for another 4 minutes.

◀ **NOTE:** *The recipe can be prepared ahead to this point. Ed.*

To assemble, reheat the sauce if necessary. Drain pears. Spoon the vanilla ice cream onto the toasted slices and top each one with a pear. Spoon the warm chocolate sauce over the pears and garnish each with a verbena or mint leaf.

NOTES: *The poaching syrup can be reused—it can even be frozen. These servings are very generous. For the end of a heavy meal, you might want to halve the recipe, or use it to serve 8. Cut the pieces of brioche in half and round the edges. Serve ½ pear per person.*

Gâteau au chocolat de Maman Guérard

Michel Guérard's Mother's Chocolate Cake

NOTE: *This dessert is essentially a chocolate mousse. Some of the mousse mixture is baked to form a cake, and the rest is left to set and then used as frosting—an admirably simple and delicious plan. Ed.*

To serve 6 to 8:

10	ounces semisweet chocolate
10	ounces butter
9	egg yolks
1⅓	cups sugar
5	egg whites
¼	cup rum (optional)

10-inch cake pan

Preheat the oven to 325° F.

Melt the chocolate with the butter in the top of a double boiler. Whisk the egg yolks with the sugar until the mixture is pale and creamy. Stir the chocolate mixture into the yolk mixture and blend well. Beat the egg whites until stiff and fold them into the chocolate mixture.

Butter and flour the cake pan, pour in ⅔ of the mixture, and bake it in the preheated oven for 1 hour. Unmold it onto a serving plate and let it cool completely. Sprinkle the cake with the rum and then frost it with the remaining chocolate mixture.

NOTE: This cake will keep for 1 week in the refrigerator if it is sprinkled with rum before it is frosted.

Pudding au coulis de framboises

Bread Pudding with Raspberry Sauce

To serve 6:

2   heaping tablespoons golden raisins

2   tablespoons rum

4   tablespoons butter, softened

⅓   pound brioche or other rich egg bread, sliced ¼ inch thick

¼   cup sugar

CUSTARD:

2   cups milk

1   vanilla bean, split in half lengthwise

3   eggs

2   egg yolks

⅔   cup sugar

1½   recipes raspberry sauce *(page 209)*

Large gratin dish

Let the raisins macerate in the rum for 30 minutes.

Butter the brioche and arrange the slices, buttered side up, on a baking sheet. Sprinkle the ¼ cup sugar over the buttered slices and toast them under the broiler until lightly browned.

Preheat the oven to 425° F.

CUSTARD:

In a saucepan, bring the milk to a boil with the vanilla bean. In a medium bowl, whisk together the eggs, egg yolks, sugar, and the rum from the raisins. Strain in part of the scalded milk, whisk, strain in the rest of the milk, and whisk well. Discard the vanilla bean.

Arrange a layer of the toast, browned side down, in the gratin dish, sprinkle with the macerated raisins, and then layer in the remaining slices of toast. Pour the hot custard over the toast. Set the gratin dish in a baking pan somewhat larger than the dish and add water to the pan to come halfway up the side of the gratin dish. Bake in the preheated oven for 30 minutes.

Meanwhile, make the raspberry sauce and chill.

When the pudding is set, remove it from the oven and let cool completely. Serve it directly from the gratin dish, accompanied by the chilled raspberry sauce.

Recettes de base

BASIC RECIPES

Fond blanc de volaille I

Chicken Stock

To make 3 quarts:

6	pounds chicken carcasses, cut up, or a large stewing hen
3	carrots, sliced
½	pound mushrooms, sliced
3	shallots, chopped
2	leeks, most of the green part cut off, well washed
1	rib celery
2	garlic cloves, crushed
1¼	cups white wine
4½	quarts water
2	onions, each stuck with a clove
	Bouquet garni

Put the cut-up chicken carcasses in a soup kettle with the carrots, mushrooms, shallots, leeks, celery, and garlic. Add the white wine and boil for 15 minutes to evaporate the alcohol. Then add the water, onions, and bouquet garni. Simmer, partially covered, for about 3 hours, skimming periodically.

Strain the stock, let cool, and then refrigerate, covered. When the stock has chilled, remove the fat from the surface.

Fond de volaille II

Short-Cut Chicken Stock

To make 3 cups:

3½ cups canned chicken broth

1   cup water

1   onion, chopped

1   carrot, chopped

1   rib celery, chopped

1   leek, white part only, well washed and sliced

2   mushrooms, chopped

Small bouquet garni

If you are making a chicken dish the same day, you may also have available the gizzard, heart, and neck, plus wing tips and fresh chicken bones. Add these to the ingredients.

Combine everything in a saucepan and simmer, partially covered, over low heat for 30 minutes. Strain the stock, let it cool, and then refrigerate, covered. When chilled, even this simple stock will probably have a thin layer of fat on the surface, which should be removed.

NOTE: *This stock is significantly different from the real thing in that it contains no natural gelatine. Ed.*

Fond ou fumet de poisson I

Fish Stock

To make 1 quart:

2   pounds heads and bones of fresh white fish
    (see **NOTE***)*, broken up

2   tablespoons butter

2   tablespoons peanut oil

1   large onion, sliced

4   mushrooms, sliced

1   shallot, chopped

6   tablespoons white wine

5   cups water

    Bouquet garni

NOTE: *The French recipe calls for the bones and heads of specific fish, such as Dover sole for its superior flavor, turbot, brill, and whiting. However, what really matters is that the fish be fresh and their flesh white and that you not use the trimmings of oily fish such as salmon, mackerel, bluefish, etc. Ed.*

Soak the bones and heads for 15 minutes in cold water and then drain. Gently heat the butter and oil in a large saucepan, add the vegetables and fish bones and heads, and cook all together over low heat for 5 minutes without letting them brown. Add the wine and boil for 15 minutes to evaporate the alcohol. Add the water and bouquet garni and simmer, partially covered, skimming periodically, for 20 minutes.

Strain the fish stock, let cool, and store, covered, in the refrigerator.

Fumet de poisson II

Short-Cut Fish Stock

To make 1 pint:

1	teaspoon olive oil
1	carrot, chopped
2	shallots, chopped
¼	cup white wine
2	cups bottled clam juice
1	cup water
2	mushrooms, sliced
	Bouquet garni, including 1 clove and 4 peppercorns

In a saucepan, heat the olive oil, add the carrot and shallots, and cook over medium heat, stirring often, until the vegetables begin to brown. Add the wine and simmer for several minutes to evaporate the alcohol. Then add all the remaining ingredients and simmer, partially covered, for 20 minutes.

Strain the stock, let it cool, and store, covered, in the refrigerator.

NOTE: *This stock is significantly different from the real thing in that it contains no natural gelatine. Ed.*

Court-bouillon I

Court-Bouillon

To make 1½ quarts:

2	carrots, thinly sliced
1	leek, white part only, well washed and thinly sliced
	8-inch piece celery, thinly sliced
4	green onions or 1 white onion, thinly sliced
2	shallots, thinly sliced
2	cups white wine
1½	quarts water
1½	tablespoons salt
5	thin strips lemon zest
2	garlic cloves, unpeeled
25	green peppercorns
	Bouquet garni, including 1 clove and a piece of fresh fennel

In a saucepan set over medium heat, cook the sliced vegetables, covered, for 5 minutes so they give off their liquid. Then add the remaining ingredients and simmer, covered, for 20 minutes.

Strain, cool and store, covered, in the refrigerator.

Court-bouillon II

Simple Court-Bouillon

To make 1½ quarts:

1½   quarts water

2   cups white wine

2   carrots, sliced

1   onion, sliced

Bouquet garni

1½   tablespoons salt

20   peppercorns

Put all the ingredients except the peppercorns in a large saucepan and simmer, covered, for 15 minutes. Add the peppercorns and cook another 5 minutes.

Strain, cool and store, covered, in the refrigerator.

Beurre blanc

White Butter Sauce

To make 1 cup:

¼   cup white wine

¼   cup white-wine vinegar

1   large shallot, finely chopped

½   pound cold butter, cut into 16 pieces

Salt and pepper

In a heavy saucepan combine the wine, vinegar, and shallot and cook over medium heat, uncovered, until the shallot has softened and nearly all the liquid has evaporated.

Turn down to the lowest possible heat and whisk in the pieces of cold butter 1 at a time, adding each one just as the previous piece has nearly been absorbed. The butter will soften, but not melt completely, and the mixture will become a creamy sauce. As you add more pieces of cold butter, you may find that you must raise the heat a little to maintain the temperature of the sauce; it should be just barely warm to the finger. Add salt and pepper to taste before serving. The *beurre blanc* can be strained to remove the shallot, but personally I leave the shallot in to preserve the rustic authenticity of this sauce.

NOTE: *To hold the sauce briefly, put the saucepan in a larger pan of luke-warm, not hot, water. Beurre blanc will congeal if it is not given some warmth, but it will melt over hot water. Ed.*

LEMON or LIME BUTTER SAUCE can be made by adding 1 tablespoon short, needle-fine strips of lemon or lime zest, first blanched in boiling water, just before serving.

Sauce hollandaise

Hollandaise Sauce

To make 1 cup:

3   egg yolks
1   tablespoon water
    Salt
6   ounces butter, softened to room temperature
1   tablespoon lemon juice

In a heavy saucepan, whisk together the yolks, water, and a good pinch of salt. Set the saucepan over very low heat and whisk constantly until the mixture thickens and becomes creamy. Now, still whisking, add the butter bit by bit. The sauce is ready when the last piece of butter has been absorbed and the whole is thickened but not heavy. Add the lemon juice. Use immediately or keep warm for a short time set in a pan of warm water.

NOTE: The essential point in making a hollandaise is the whisking, which equalizes the temperature of the egg yolks as they coagulate and also beats air into the sauce to lighten it.

Sauce coulis de tomates fraîches

Fresh Tomato Sauce

To make 1 cup:

1	teaspoon olive oil
1	shallot, chopped
½	small garlic clove, unpeeled but crushed
¾	cup chopped fresh tomatoes *(page 204)*
1	teaspoon tomato paste
	Bouquet garni
½	cup chicken stock *(pages 194–195)*
	Salt and pepper

Heat the oil in a saucepan and in it gently cook the shallot. Add the garlic, tomatoes, tomato paste, bouquet garni, and chicken stock. Simmer for 20 minutes.

Remove the bouquet garni, purée the mixture in a food processor or an electric blender, and season it lightly to taste with salt and pepper. If the sauce is too thin, pour it back into the saucepan and simmer it again until it is reduced but not heavy. Serve either hot or cold.

Sauce coulis d'asperges minceur

Minceur Asparagus Sauce

To serve 4:

¾ pound fresh asparagus
½ cup chicken stock *(pages 194–195)*
   Salt and pepper
1 teaspoon *crème fraîche (page 206)*

Break off and discard the tough ends of the asparagus stalks. Cut the asparagus into 1-inch pieces and cook in boiling salted water until soft enough to pierce easily with a fork, about 10 minutes. Drain and purée the pieces in a food processor or an electric blender with the chicken stock, salt and pepper to taste, and the *crème fraîche*. Reheat gently before serving.

Sauce coulis d'artichauts minceur

Minceur Artichoke Sauce

To serve 4:

3 small artichokes (1½ to 1¾ pounds in all)
   Juice of 1 lemon
½ cup chicken stock *(pages 194–195)*
   Salt and pepper
1 teaspoon *crème fraîche (page 206)*

Cut off and discard the stems of the artichokes. Cook the artichokes, covered, for 45 minutes in gently boiling water, salted and acidulated with the lemon juice. Drain and put in cold water to cool.

Remove all the leaves and scoop out the chokes. Cut the artichoke bottoms in pieces and purée them in a food processor or an electric blender with the chicken stock, salt and pepper to taste, and *crème fraîche*. Reheat gently before serving.

Sauce vinaigrette gourmande

Vinaigrette Gourmande

To make ½ cup:

1½   tablespoons lemon juice
1½   tablespoons sherry vinegar
     Salt and pepper
2½   tablespoons peanut oil
2½   tablespoons olive oil
 1   tablespoon each finely chopped fresh tarragon and chervil *(see page 212 for substitutions)*

In a small bowl, combine the lemon juice, vinegar, and some salt and pepper and mix well to dissolve the salt. Gradually whisk in the peanut and olive oils. Stir in the chopped fresh herbs, taste, and add more salt and pepper if needed.

Sauce vinaigrette minceur

Minceur Vinaigrette

To make ½ cup:

1   tablespoon olive oil

5   tablespoons chicken stock *(pages 194–195)*

1   garlic clove

½   teaspoon each finely chopped fresh tarragon, chervil, and basil *(see pages 211–212 for substitutions)*

1   tablespoon lemon juice

1   tablespoon sherry vinegar

    Salt and pepper

Combine the olive oil, stock, garlic, and herbs in a small bowl and let them marinate for 2 hours. Add the lemon juice, vinegar, and salt and pepper and mix well.

Tomate fraîche concassée

Chopped Fresh Tomatoes

To make 1½ quarts:

3   pounds ripe tomatoes

Bring a large pot of water to a boil. Cut out the little stem and green core from each tomato, drop the tomatoes into the boiling water, and boil just long enough to loosen the skins, about 15 seconds. Drain them, cool under cold running water, and peel. Cut the peeled tomatoes in half crosswise and squeeze each half to remove the seeds and excess juice. Chop coarsely and, if not using immediately, store, covered, in the refrigerator.

Tomate concassée cuite

Cooked Chopped Fresh Tomatoes

To make 1 quart:

3   pounds ripe tomatoes
1   teaspoon olive oil
2   shallots, chopped
2   garlic cloves, unpeeled but crushed
    Small bouquet garni
    Salt and pepper

Peel, seed, and chop the tomatoes as described in the preceding recipe. Heat the olive oil in a large saucepan, add the shallots, and cook slowly until they soften and brown lightly. Add the tomatoes, garlic, bouquet garni, and salt and pepper. Partially cover the pan, lower the heat, and simmer for 30 minutes.

Remove the garlic and bouquet garni and add salt and pepper if needed. If not used immediately, store, covered, in the refrigerator.

Crème fraîche

Crème Fraîche

To make 1¼ cups:

1 cup heavy cream
¼ cup sour cream or yogurt

Mix both ingredients together, cover, and leave at room temperature for 8 to 12 hours. Stir again and refrigerate, covered, for at least 24 hours before using.

Fromage blanc

Fromage Blanc

To make 1½ cups:

1½ cups low-fat diet ricotta cheese
¼ cup low-fat yogurt
Pinch salt

Purée all the ingredients in a food processor or an electric blender until absolutely smooth and refrigerate, covered, at least 12 hours before using.

La pâte feuilletée

Puff Pastry

To make 1½ pounds:

1¾ cups flour *(see* **NOTES***)*
½ cup cold water
1 teaspoon salt
3½ tablespoons butter, softened
½ pound plus 2 tablespoons cold butter

MAKING THE DOUGH:

Method I (by hand): Put the flour on the work surface and use your fingers to make a well in the center. The work surface should be visible in the middle of a ring of flour. Put the water, salt, and the softened butter in the well. Use the tips of your fingers to mix these ingredients together while gradually incorporating the flour. Gather the dough into a ball.

Method II (with a food processor): Put the flour, water, salt, and softened butter into the food processor. Run the machine until the ingredients form a ball, about 30 seconds.

Flatten the ball of dough slightly and use a sharp knife to slit the surface like a tic-tac-toe board, with 2 shallow, parallel cuts and then 2 more across the first cuts. Refrigerate the dough, covered, for 2 hours before rolling out.

INCORPORATING THE BUTTER:

Put the cold butter on a piece of plastic wrap or parchment paper and cover it with another piece. Using a rolling pin, tap the butter to flatten it to an approximately 6-inch square.

Lightly flour the work surface, take the dough from the refrigerator, and roll it out to an approximately 10-inch square. Put the flattened butter in the center of the dough; the corners of the butter square should point to the sides of the square of dough. Fold the dough over the butter, completely enclosing it in an envelope of dough.

Lightly flour the work surface again and roll the dough out to a rectangle approximately 10 by 20 inches, about ⅜ inch thick. Roll continually away from you to lengthen the dough; do not roll crosswise. If the dough tears, exposing the butter, patch it with a sprinkling of flour. Fold the dough in thirds as you would fold a business letter.

Turn the dough so that the folds are perpendicular to you. Repeat the rolling and folding exactly as above. Refrigerate, covered, for 30 minutes before rolling it out again.

Remove the dough from the refrigerator, repeat the process of rolling and folding 2 more times as above, and again refrigerate for 30 minutes.

Remove the dough from the refrigerator and give it 2 final rollings and foldings to make 6 in all. It is now ready to use.

Extra pastry dough can be rolled out, cut into any desired shapes, layered with plastic wrap, and frozen. Use directly from the freezer rather than defrosting first. Scraps can be stacked together and used like any other pastry dough.

NOTES: While in New York, I developed a variation of this dough for use in the United States. Although the recipe given above will work very well, a slightly lighter puff pastry was obtained by using a mixture of flours in the proportion of 3 parts all-purpose flour to 1 part cake flour. When making puff pastry, both the dough and the butter rolled into it must be cold. In hot weather, or in a warm kitchen, it is best to cool the work surface by putting trays of ice on it for 30 minutes before rolling out the dough. When cutting puff pastry, use only a large, very sharp knife with a straight-edge blade. Cut the dough with one quick, clean stroke; do not pull the knife through the dough or squeeze the edges of the dough by pressing down too slowly or else the edges of the dough will not rise properly. Why does puff pastry puff? Like magic, a piece of dough that is nearly paper thin suddenly rises as much as 20 times its original height when placed in the oven. This "miracle" has baffled many amateur chefs, when in fact it is easy to explain. When the dough is rolled out, alternating layers of dough and butter are formed. When baked, the butter sizzles and pushes up the layer of dough just above it. Simultaneously, the water in the dough turns to steam, which tries to escape, pushing up the layer above it. The result is the miracle of perfect puff pastry.

Sauce coulis de framboises, fraises, ou cassis

Raspberry, Strawberry, or Black Currant Sauce

To serve 4:

1 pint fresh or ½ pound frozen raspberries, strawberries, or black currants (*see* **NOTE**)

½ cup sugar, or to taste

Juice of 1 lemon, or to taste

NOTE: *If using frozen fruit, allow it to thaw completely before making the sauce, and add sugar, if necessary, to taste. Ed.*

Purée all the ingredients in a food processor or an electric blender, strain, and refrigerate.

Sauce coulis de framboises, fraises, ou cassis minceur

Minceur Raspberry, Strawberry, or Black Currant Sauce

Make as the preceding recipe, but substitute artificial sweetener equivalent to ½ cup sugar. If using frozen fruit, it must, of course, be unsweetened.

Sauce coulis d'abricots

Apricot Sauce

To serve 4:

12   fresh apricots, halved and pitted, or an equal
      number of canned apricots in syrup

5   tablespoons sugar, for fresh apricots

1   vanilla bean, split open lengthwise

1   tablespoon dark rum

If using fresh apricots, put them, 1 cup of water, the sugar, and vanilla bean in a saucepan. Bring to a boil, lower the heat, and simmer, uncovered, stirring often, for about 25 minutes. The liquid should reduce to two-thirds its original volume and the mixture should look somewhat like thin apricot preserves. If using canned apricots, simmer ⅔ cup of their syrup with the vanilla bean, covered, for 10 minutes and add the apricots.

Take out the vanilla bean and pour the mixture into a food processor or an electric blender, add the rum, and whir until well mixed. Serve warm or cold.

Sauce coulis d'abricots minceur

Minceur Apricot Sauce

Make as the preceding recipe, but use fresh apricots or unsweetened canned apricots and artificial sweetener equivalent to 5 tablespoons sugar. Omit the rum.

EDITORS' NOTES ON INGREDIENTS

A basic **bouquet garni** includes parsley, a sprig of dried thyme, and a bay leaf. Surround the thyme and bay leaf with parsley stems and then wind a piece of string around the herbs from one end to the other and tie to make a compact bundle that won't come apart during cooking.

Quatre épices, literally four spices, is a mixture of ground white pepper, nutmeg, ginger, and cloves that is sold ready-mixed according to various formulas. You can make your own starting with 1 tablespoon white pepper, ¾ teaspoon nutmeg, ¾ teaspoon ginger, and ¼ teaspoon cloves and adjusting proportions to suit your taste.

For citrus **zest,** pare off only the aromatic, colored part of the peeling, none of the bitter white pith underneath.

SUBSTITUTIONS:

You can be sure that, if Michel Guérard were cooking where you are, he would not toss out all the dishes in his repertoire for which he couldn't get the ingredients that he uses in France. So rather than not try a recipe, make reasonable substitutions such as the following:

If thin, young **asparagus** is unavailable, use regular asparagus and cook it a little longer than specified, or use just the tips.

If it's the wrong time of year for **baby vegetables,** use larger ones cut in pieces and made more attractive by paring into smooth ovals.

For fresh **basil,** use basil leaves preserved in oil. If you grow your own or can buy in quantity during the season, putting basil up yourself is simple. Just strip the leaves from the stems, wash and dry them, and then pack as many as possible into a jar and pour oil over to cover, rapping the jar on the table to get the oil down to the bottom. The basil will keep for weeks in the refrigerator and can be frozen for longer storage. The oil is delicious in salad dressings and on pasta.

Chervil is similar to parsley but more delicate. If the main ingredients in a recipe are strongly flavored, such as broccoli or cod, use an equal quantity of parsley for the chervil. For milder flavored dishes, you might want to cut the quantity of parsley in half.

If you can't buy the slightly sour, nutty-flavored **crème fraîche** and haven't time to make a batch, heavy cream can be used.

Many **fish** recipes are virtually interchangeable. Use whatever is fresh and good locally, just making sure you substitute the same type—a lean, white fish when that is the kind specified, a rich full-flavored fish when that is the type for which the recipe was developed.

Flat-leaf parsley is stronger than the more readily available curly parsley, so you can use somewhat more curly when substituting it for the flat-leaf.

Yogurt can usually be substituted for **fromage blanc.**

If **leeks** are unavailable or too expensive, onions can be substituted when the leeks are used as flavoring rather than as a major ingredient. Use a quarter of an onion for each leek.

Good **puff pastry** is available now in specialty shops, but do try to find pastry made entirely with real butter. Frozen supermarket puff pastry works well, but it is not made entirely with butter. Follow the package instructions for defrosting.

Green onions or scallions can substitute for **shallots;** two green onions per shallot. Or you can even use a slice of regular onion.

For fresh **tarragon,** substitute tarragon preserved in vinegar, rinsed off before using. This is available in jars in specialty food shops or can be made by immersing tarragon branches in any good vinegar, and the vinegar just benefits from the process. Tarragon in vinegar keeps indefinitely at room temperature.

Dried thyme leaves can be substituted for dried **thyme sprigs**; about a quarter teaspoon per sprig.

INDEX